The Secrets of High
Self-Esteem

The Secrets of High Self-Esteem

Your 21 Day Guide to Success

Adam Eason

www.adam-eason.com

Adam Eason
www.adam-eason.com
Copyright 2006
Adam Eason
All Rights Reserved

**The Secrets of High Self-Esteem:
Your 21 Day Guide to Success**

Includes Bibliographic References

ISBN: 0-9709321-6-2
ISBN: 978-0-9709321-6-7

Self-Help Techniques

Printed in the United States of America
Network 3000 Publishing
3432 Denmark Avenue #108
Eagan, Minnesota 55123
USA
(612) 616-0732

This Book is dedicated to Ben Eason.

My teacher, supporter, best friend and of course;
beloved brother.

He makes me laugh like no other can and makes me
feel good about being myself.

Contents

Introduction

My 30th birthday was the single hottest day in the UK that year. I mean it was hot. I am in Mortehoe, a small village in North Devon on the west coast of England. I am on a campsite late evening, the air is warm, the sky is clear and with no real light pollution, the stars are really twinkling. I am sat in a chair, my face glowing with the heat from the days sunshine and the glowing embers of the barbecues beside me. One of my best friends Jo said to me 'Wipe the marshmallow off your face . . .'. You know how much fun I was having!

I am encircled by a group of approximately 35 of my close friends from various chapters of my life.

We are having a weekend camping, loads of my friends had celebrated their 30th in the past few years and so I decided to get away from pubs and clubs to celebrate my 30th. I wanted to do something different and head out to the coast; we had been surfing, playing games on the beach, eating, drinking and generally having a ball.

One of my very close friend's was nicknamed Bunty; Bunty was a cartoon character in The Roy of the Rovers football magazine when we were kids. Bunty was a character that played football and when he fell over he bounced up again, that was him alright, he bounced whenever we played football and always seemed to land on his feet. Anyway, he had had to drink a lot of water and have a sit down when we had lunchtime drinks due to the red colour of his back. More sun cream for Bunty next time. When he took his vest off, it looked like he was still wearing it on account of him having red skin everywhere where the vest had not been covering. In later years we went on holiday together with some other close friends and when he had still not learnt his lesson and was red skinned again, we re-nicknamed him 'Burnty'.

Anyway, I digress. I had strolled lazily back from the showers and some serious grooming for the night ahead, well, as serious as you can do in the steamy shower rooms on a campsite and I was heading in the direction of where all our tents were pitched. I had a very old Volkswagen Campervan that is 6 months older than I am and I loved going camping in her; beautiful machines those, mine was racing green, original interior and was imaginatively named 'Bertha' on account of her being a 4 berth campervan.

So, as I walked back, the views were something special. Overlooking green sloping hills to the beaches and the sea. The immediate coastline had big rock stalagmites coming out of the sea that were casting silhouettes across the cliffs and the sun was setting on the surface of the sea; stunning. Absolutely stunning.

As I arrived back, all changed and smelling wonderful again, I was greeted with a cheer by all my friends that had congregated, tied balloons to Bertha and instructed me to sit down for a birthday surprise. Now, if you have friends like mine, you start getting nervous when they say things like that. I sat down and Roy, one of my friends from Bournemouth, announced that everyone had been emailing each other behind my back that week and they had decided that they would all bring something along to the evening that reminded them of me and that they would tell the story that went with it.

It is at this point that I am scared, my girlfriend is here and I am not sure if she knows everything about me just yet and I am not sure if I want her to know everything!

My best friend from university Ed, told everybody a story about the time him and I pretended to be bar owners and conned our way into the set of the UK's most popular TV soap opera, Coronation Street, for a free drinks promotion and were given free drinks for a day and a night. He gave me a photo of him and I, arm in arm, in the set of the Rovers Return bar from during that day.

One of my best friends from my hometown, Toby, (we called him Spanner because he was into cars and once smacked himself in the head with a spanner and came out to the pub with a scar on his forehead) told a story about the time him and I and a couple of others had jumped into a taxi at the end of a night out and told the driver where to go, only to find out half way through the lengthy journey that he was not actually a taxi driver and was too scared to tell us.

A great friend of mine Nick, had told of how I made all the guys at his pre-wedding stag night wear leopard skin thongs outside their trousers and so he brought me a new one that went comfortably over my trousers and looked great at the campsite.

My brother had made a 30th birthday T-shirt for me with a picture of me wearing a wig on it and I had to wear the T-shirt for the night; I actually wore it all weekend.

The night went on like this, person upon person took turns to stand up and tell me about how much fun they had had with me and the laughter from everyone made me giddy and emotional.

Emotional, because my mind now wandered back to several years earlier in the late 1980s. I am lying on my bed staring at the ceiling and it is blurred. In fact, the artex ceiling is moving, it is slopping around looking to me like someone stirring paint in a pot. The reason for my strange vision is that in the last half hour of this September day in 1989, I have just taken a large cocktail of pain killers, slcohol and anti-depressant tablets. My stomach is feeling weird as you would expect, in fact it is gurgling. I am thinking to myself that I am dying.

I had not become the superstar footballer that I was tipped to be, I had not got that hotshot job that my educational excellence had anticipated or become any of the amazing things that all my school teachers thought I would. In fact, in my eyes, having not made any impression on the world apart from doing poorly, I have had enough of being no-one, with no value of myself, not living up to expectations and am now committing suicide.

The only thing that stopped me from dying, in my opinion, was my Mum finding me half unconscious and then having to force myself to be desperately sick in the hope of recovering.

This is not something that many people have encountered I am guessing, but let me tell you this; from my experience, the dreamy idea of drifting off comfortably at your own hand is not as easy as you may think. Faced with the reality of dying, in a very surreal experience, I am now imagining my own funeral when in the real world my Mum has arrived home and starts calling my name.

Imagining her there in tears if she discovered me like this, I start remembering stories of how proud my Mum and Dad were when I became deputy head boy at school. I remembered my grandmother telling me about the time, prior to my birth, how my Dad had told everyone that he was going to have a red haired son and on the day I was born how proud he was. I remember my Dad driving me all over the country and watching me play football every weekend in all kinds of weather conditions and how involved he would be and how he was with me when I played well and scored goals. I remember how my brother used to happily follow me around when we were toddlers and how in adult life we made a pact to be the best man at each others weddings while hugging.

But, on my bed, the lights went out for me. I think I am dying.

Suddenly, I can hear crystal clear, sharp sounds.

The next few days were a blur to me. I am looking at a counsellor. She is asking me all sorts of questions and telling me things and despite her very pleasant demeanour and agreeable smile, I am finding the discussion moribund. I have no interest in what she is saying and very little of what she is doing or telling me is of any value to me right there and then. She just wants to discuss my life, which I tend to think is obviously problematic right now.

I spent some weeks recovering physically and then some months recovering mentally and must admit that I still experience times now when I feel the pain of that time in my life. As the years ticked by from then onwards, I had never truly stopped and examined my life. My natural coping mechanism was to bury my head and not spend too much more time analysing my life, not keep regurgitating past pain. Instead, to move forward; I studied and studied and learnt more about lots of ways to feel good about myself. I went on courses all over the world to train to help others that had been near the end like I had. I read books on a wide variety of self-help topics to learn how to excel and develop myself for the better, I had set up my own business and was pushing on forward. It was a long journey, that I am still not even sure that I have reached the end of.

But there I was, on my 30th birthday, on the most beautiful campsite, staring at the faces of my friends all looking at me and laughing and smiling and beside me is a growing pile of pictures, toys, cards, items that would mean nothing to most people, that all have a connection between someone and me.

As I look at those things, with their associated memories, it is getting cooler and some people are going to bed, some going into the village to the pub and I said I would join them shortly. I had never realised the impact that some of the most innocuous actions and things that I had done had been imprinted on the minds of others. One of my friends from home Jo came over to me and said 'I am so sorry for not having told a story Adam, you know what I'm like; I don't like getting up in front of people'. 'You know that we all love you anyway don't you . . .' In a real matter of fact way as she walked over to her tent and began zipping it up.

'I do now . . .' I thought with my chin wobbling all over the place. I went and sat in my campervan for a couple of minutes and cried. In fact I cried so hard, that I had to stuff my beach towel over my mouth to muffle the sounds.

When Jo said that, it reminded me of my Mum saying to me back then 'We do love you, you do know that don't you'. This was the beginning of the development of my self-esteem. I know now why I failed miserably in my attempt to end things. To this day, I do my best to tell my friends and family that I love them and tell them of the impact things they do have on me, because I know that kind of stuff spreads into the lives of others and might just help someone develop their own sense of self without having to go through such traumatic times. I recommend you do the same.

The main purpose of me telling you this is that as I write these pages today, I am author of a best selling book on self-hypnosis, I have starred in a prime time BBC1 documentary series for TV, my personal development audio programmes and hypnosis programmes sell all over the world, I speak internationally and regularly appear in magazines discussing my work. I have a long waiting list for people to consult with me and individuals and companies seek me out to do so. I consider myself to have come a very long way. That journey would not have been possible if I had not been able to help myself to get in control of my brain and my experience of life and build my own sense of self-esteem. The life I am leading today would have been impossible without me first developing my sense of self and nurturing the relationship I have with myself.

This book represents a concise, step by step guide on how to create self-esteem, examine how you function and respond to life, how to be happier and happier, enhance your self-esteem and how to use it to excel and create the life you want and are fulfilled by.

This book includes everything that I used over a number of years to establish and develop my own self-esteem and it is all yours in the next 21 days.

I thank you for allowing me to share it all with you and hope you enjoy the journey as much as I did.

How to Read this Book

Let me tell you about the guy that I wrote about at the beginning of my last book; I had a man referred to me once by one of London's top psychiatrists, he strolled into my consulting rooms and let out an enormous and dramatic sigh and slumped into the chair.

'I am taking seroxat, I was on Prozac. I have been diagnosed by several doctors as having clinical depression for the last twelve years and have been seeing one of London's top psychiatrists for the last 5 years. He referred me to you. I think I am going to be very difficult for you to deal with' he said.

I could not help but laugh. Right there in front of him. He frowned and looked at me and said in a less apathetic, more serious tone 'Don't you think you should be taking my problems a bit more seriously Mr Eason?'

'No way,' I replied. 'You are taking your problems too seriously for the both of us. If I wanted to be really good at being depressed, I would take it really seriously. There are other therapists around here who will pander to you in that way and take your problems very seriously; but I won't.'

We both sat for 3 very long seconds of silence.

'Look . . .' I said, 'I run marathons, half-marathons and other long distance races regularly and I consider myself to have a lot of endurance. But that is nothing compared to the level of endurance that you must have to have gone to the same psychiatrist for 5 years! Having gone for two years and having little success, what on earth possessed you to go for another 3 years?'

I knew that he and I were making stunning progress when he came into my consulting rooms to meet me four weeks later and he made a joke at my expense, that's right, he openly mocked me. I knew he was making progress. He was feeling better about himself, more confident and we had set him free of lots of other things that were holding him back from being himself.

Firstly, let me explain that this book is punctuated with my own particular brand of humour. Lots of it is tongue in cheek, please bear that in mind. I like to have fun; personal development should be fun and really is fun. Every single page of this book is written with that in mind, so please be aware of that if you think the manner is unusual from time to time or that I am labouring a point from time to time.

Please just allow yourself to use this book in a way that resonates smoothly with you. There may be some aspects of it that you don't agree with or don't like, where as other parts seem to resonate with you deeply and wonderfully. The aim of this book is to facilitate, *not dictate* your experience and skills as you take control of your brain and learn how to use it more effectively to have more self-esteem.

I have been told a certain story several times by differing people as I have made changes in my life and it goes a bit like this:

A young man is running down the street with a violin under his arm. He frantically stops and asks an old gentleman nearby 'How do I get to the Albert Hall?' The old man looks at the desperate young man and somberly replies, 'Practice, practice, practice.'

Personal development and enhancing self-esteem can be just the same. I spend a lot of time each day studying, practising, and keeping my brain in optimum working order to ensure I feel happy and well. Athletes train and practice their skills and we do it with most other things that we want to become not only competent at, but excellent at. When you become excellent at using your brain, then enhancing your self-esteem is an inevitability.

Follow this book methodically and in the order that it is presented. It is in the order that it is for specific reasons. Learn about yourself, how your mind works and how to develop it beyond your wildest dreams to create success and happiness.

Be relaxed when reading this book, and though it is for use in 21 days, read it often again and again and pick up things that may not have sunk in the first time, be sure to take notes and jot down ideas and when reading allow the information to flow over you without giving it too much conscious analysis. Your conscious mind will get its share of learning from the projects that you complete with each day.

Allow the information to wash over you in the same way that waves of warm soothing water wash over your feet when you paddle in the sea on holiday. Allow it to access your deeper unconscious mind so that the things you are learning about become inherent in your life and so that you do not have to think about employing these skills and abilities consciously, they just become part of the way in which you naturally are and your subsequent self-esteem is just as natural.

Each day you are going to be asked to do a project. This will consolidate that days learning and firmly embed it in your mind. The most success will be achieved by those that do complete these exercises. Do not allow this information to simply be read and stored within you along with all the other stuff that you learnt and do not use.

Do the projects! Excuse the Sergeant Major approach here, but it is so very important. Notice how the daily projects make you feel and how that when you actually 'do' things they become far more usable than the theory of doing them. I want to help to show you how to really do some amazing things with your life and I can only do that if you follow the instructions in the correct order and do the projects. I thank you in advance for doing that and I know you will thank me in the long run when you have done them.

Please ensure that you do all the exercises as they are going to be what stretches your brain to do different things and be open to further increasing your self-esteem. If you allow yourself to just read this book and take the entire process too easily, then your level of self-esteem enhancement will be minimal. If you take the required actions, you open yourself to unbounded levels of self-esteem as your brain has some physical reality and experience to combine within your neurology and your success is in the post. One of my favourite authors Napoleon Hill wrote:

'Your ship can NOT come in unless you first send it out'

How many ships have you sent out today? By completing the projects in this book at the end of each days learning, you are sending another ship out. By the end of this book you will have sent a lot of ships out there and they will soon return brimming with a renewed sense of self-worth.

The actions that you take throughout this book are going to seal your success. If you wanted to train for a marathon, you would not run ten metres a day in preparation would you? You need to push yourself and accept some responsibility for what you are doing. Start by making sure you do each day's project as thoroughly as possible. Some of the projects are going to take some time and others will be considerably less challenging, please remember this throughout the entire book; each project is just as important as the others, they are all there for a very specific reason. Do you think I have made that point strongly enough?

If you have some particular issue that you wish to deal with, a reason that you invested in this book, you might be tempted to race to a section that deals with it more precisely. Resist the urge to do this. Please read this book in the order it is presented, I can't stress this point enough and that is why I have repeated this point in this opening. This is a guide to successfully growing your self-esteem. Allow yourself to be guided correctly and you will discover some wonders.

I wish you all the very best with this book and I just know that having come this far, you really can achieve the kind of self-esteem that you deserve, and make the changes and updates that you want to make or develop in the way you want to or achieve the results that you know you are capable of.

For your information, the quotes under each days beginning are simply quotes relating to the number of that day, they are not directly related to the content of that days learning.

What is Self-Esteem?

You can't touch it, but it affects how you feel. You can't see it, but it is there when you look at yourself in the mirror. You can't hear it, but it is there affecting every kind of communication you engage in.

To understand self-esteem, it helps to examine the term into two words. Let's take a look at the word esteem first. Esteem is a fancy word for thinking that someone or something is important or valuing that person or thing. For example, if you really admire your friend's father because he does a lot of work for charity, it means you hold him in high esteem. And the special award for the most valuable player on a team is often called an esteemed trophy. This means the trophy stands for an important accomplishment.

And self means, of course, yourself! So when you put these two words together, it is far easier to understand what self-esteem is. It is how much you value yourself and how important you think you are. It is how you perceive yourself and how you feel about your achievements. You are going to read in more detail what self-esteem actually is later in this book.

Self-esteem is not bragging about how great you are, it is often people who lack self-esteem who behave like that. It is much more of a quiet sense of knowing that you are worth a lot; you have value. It certainly is not about thinking you are perfect in every way – because nobody is – rather, it is simply knowing that you are worthy of being loved and accepted; primarily by yourself.

Why is Self-Esteem so Important?

Self-esteem is not like a brilliant pair of running shoes that I start drooling over when I see them reviewed in a running magazine and start having desirous thoughts about, they are things that I would love to have but do not have to have. Good levels of self-esteem are important because it helps you to hold your head high and feel proud of yourself and what you can do. It gives you the courage to do new things and it gives you the power to believe in yourself. It lets you respect yourself, even if you make mistakes. It is when you respect yourself that others usually respect you, too.

Having good levels of self-esteem is also the ticket to making good choices about your mind and body. If you think you are important, especially as a child, you are far less likely to mindlessly follow the crowd and be easily led into directions that are wrong for you. When you have good self-esteem, you know that you are clever enough to make your own decisions that are for your better and higher good. You value your well-being, your safety, your feelings, your health – your entire self! Good levels of self-esteem help you to just know that every part of you is worth caring for and protecting, even without consciously having to do so.

How do Children Develop Self-Esteem?

Babies do not see themselves in a good or bad way. They are not born into this world, and the first words from their mouths are to exclaim 'I am great!' They do not go through their years of being a toddler saying things like 'Uh-Oh, this nappy makes my bum look big!' Instead, those that interact with a baby help that baby to develop self-esteem. How do they do this? They do this by continually encouraging the baby when they learn to crawl, walk, or talk for themselves. People frequently say to babies ''good job' or 'well done'. When people take good care of a baby, they are also helping that baby to feel loved and valuable which results in them feeling and being more lovable.

As children get older, they do have a more important role in developing their own self-esteem. When children have achieve-ments – like getting a good mark in an exam or making the first eleven of the football team – they have things they can be proud of. They can also be proud of having a good sense of humour or being a good friend.

A child's family and other people in his or her life – like teachers, team-mates, and classmates – can and do contribute to his or her self-esteem. They can help a child to instinctively figure out how to do things or heighten their own awareness of his or her special qualities. It is these people that you come in contact with as you develop that believe in you as a child and in turn encourage you to persevere when things may not go quite as planned at certain times in your lives. It is all part of a child's learning process to perceive themselves in a positive way, to feel proud of what they have done, and to be confident that there is a lot more they can do and be open to the good things life has to offer. You all know that things do not always go quite to this plan.

Sometimes a child will have low self-esteem as a result of their mother or father not encouraging them enough or if there is a lot of continued conflict at home. In other ways, a child's self-esteem can be weakened or damaged in the classroom. A teacher may make a child feel stupid or perhaps there is a bully who says hurtful things. These things and others can all have a detrimental effect on early levels of self-esteem, during your developmental years. Once you have learnt a particular way of believing in and perceiving yourself, it can get embedded and continue to happen on auto-pilot throughout your later years in life.

For some children, classes at school can seem so hard that they can't keep up or get the marks in class that they had hoped for. Not achieving the same results as peers within a linear academic education system can make a child feel bad about themselves and damage their self-esteem. A child's self-esteem will naturally improve when a teacher, tutor, or counsellor encourages them, is patient, and helps them get back on track with learning. When they start to do well, their self-esteem rockets!

And there are some children who have fantastic levels of self-esteem but then something happens to change that. For example, if a child's family moves into a new area and that child does not make friends right away at the new school or in the new neighbourhood, he or she might start to feel bad about themselves.

A child whose parents divorce may also find that this can affect self-esteem. He or she may feel unlovable or to blame for the divorce. It is common for a child to believe so and things can get even worse when divorced parents meet other partners. A child who feels too fat or too thin may start thinking that means he or she isn't good enough. Even going through the physiological bodily changes of puberty – something that everybody does – can affect a child's self-esteem in a variety of different ways.

Of course it is allowed, I mean it is fine to have ups and downs in your feelings, but having low self-esteem is not fine, and should not be allowed from here on. Feeling as if you are not important can make you sad, feel less than wonderful and can hold you back from doing so many things in life. Low self-esteem can keep you from making friends or can damage your learning progression in many aspects of life. Having strong self-esteem is also a very big part of growing up. As you get older it plays a more and more pivotal role in your progress professionally and personally.

As you are going to be learning, by focusing on the good things you do and all your great qualities, you learn to love and accept yourself – these are some of the main ingredients for strong self-esteem! Even if you have got room for improvement (and we all do), realising that you are valuable and important helps your self-esteem to shine in such a way that others feel it and notice it and you are going to learn how to do that during the coming days.

You may well have your own definition and your own terms of what self-esteem means to you and your life. Because you have your own ideas and personal interpretations of self-esteem, this book gives you the necessary tools to achieve whatever you consider to be your own growing sense of self in your own terms. Please ensure, though, that you reach for the stars and allow yourself to be the fullest possible expression of yourself as you want to be; be open and really take the time and invest the energy into this daily guide.

You are going to need a pen or pencil and a journal of some kind. You can, of course, use scraps of paper, but if you really want to value yourself and how you relate to yourself, then begin as you mean to go on and get yourself a nice journal and make it your self-esteem journal. Your self-esteem journal can be a record of how you began to chart your success and one day not too far into the future you can look back at these moments as having been the start of something truly amazing happening in your life. There are lots of things to be writing throughout this book and it is extremely valuable for you to notice the shifts that you are going through. Noting your progress, thoughts and the findings from the daily projects along with the projects themselves is going to be very valuable as we progress. OK, let's get cracking.

Project for the Day

You shall be getting very used to those words in bold towards the end of every day. I have a project for you to do before we get on with the daily guide. This book has some of the most modern, insightful and advanced techniques that are going to help you develop your self-esteem, but if your past experiences and learnt thought processes and behaviours keep on getting in the way of it, you are going to keep getting dragged back to where you began.

If every time you apply a new way of thinking, you unconsciously are dragged back by past experiences, then you will get nowhere. So before we begin, we need to unearth past experiences and process them all very differently. I have never liked spending too much time in the past, it certainly never really helped me when I was younger. However, I am not talking about just uncovering things from your past and rummaging around in past experiences, oh no. I do not think that would be useful to you, in fact it would just remind you of all the reasons that you arrived where you are today. I am talking about unearthing aspects of your past that may be holding you back, then processing them differently in your mind. You will never be able to erase things from your memory unless you were turned into some kind of Stepford wife, instead you want to learn how to process your behaviours and thoughts in relation to past experiences in a different and new way. In a way that means each time you think of a past experience that has been a contributory factor to maybe having a lack of self-esteem, you now allow it to drive you forward and not hold you back.

Project for today: Follow these steps
Step 1: Write down a minimum of 10 specific memories from your earlier life that you consider to have been pivotal in harming your self-esteem in any way at all. Maybe they have a strong emotional response to you or your life or someone's comments about you that have contributed to your beliefs, thoughts or habits about you and your self-esteem. Be as detailed as you can. These need to be memories that have been pivotal, in your opinion, to your recent state of mind in relation to your sense of self.

Ensure that these things are specifically related to your sense of self. This must include feelings about the people involved, your experiences, situations, what people said to you or told you. These experiences will all have emotional content that is significant and in some cases powerful and profound.

This project for today may take time but is one of the most important things you will do in this book.

Step 2: Write each memory on a separate piece of paper in your journal. If you think of more than one memory at a time always write your memories down first then return to each one individually later.

Step 3: In as much detail as possible, write about each memory. Include how you felt at the time and what people said. Write down what you saw, what you heard and what and how you felt. Describe it in as much sensory detail as possible.

Step 4: As you write about this memory write down specifically how you believe this memory influenced and shaped your self-esteem and beliefs about yourself in the present. Be sure to write down as many other ways that you think this memory could have influenced you.

Step 5: This is the key part of this project. Go ahead and assign a new and different meaning to this memory. It needs to be one that is productive and valuable to your current life and in building your self-esteem. Write this new meaning out in great detail. Basically, here you are reframing that memory into it benefiting you in some way instead of hindering you. Write out how you have benefited from it; basically reframe the entire thing so that every time you think of it, it has a new meaning that benefits you. Allow the memory to somehow allow you to grow your self-esteem.

For example, I could view my own personal experience of overdosing as a younger man as something that was selfish, harmful to others, problematic and could allow it to contribute to lessening my self-esteem. Instead I choose to view it as the catalyst that sparked my reinvention and development of my relationship with myself. I do not think of it as a happy time, that would be unrealistic, I just choose to think of it as the beginning of a new story in my life that drives me forward and spurs me on to feel good about who I am. You see how I have reframed it into something progressive? There are going to be things that you may think have no good in them what so ever, and you have to be very creative and think about how it made you stronger, think about what you would like to believe about it and just do your best to allow it to move you forward in some way.

Step 6: Run through each and every one of these memories and the new beneficial meaning you have assigned to this memory every day for the next 21 days (at least). This will ensure it forms part of your neurology and becomes an inherent part of who you are. If written down thoroughly, it can be read and re-read to get it embedded. Then each time you enter certain circumstances or situations, if you choose to remember things from the past, allow yourself to be encouraged by what you have learnt and how you are being driven by memories instead of framing them as problems that are going to repeat and make you feel lacking in self-esteem in some way.

Do your best to date your memories with your age and maybe the year they took place. These do not have to be 'bad or unhappy memories'. You can write down joyous ones as well. They just have to be things that you feel have affected the way you relate to yourself.

Once you have written your memories and dates, take some time to be sure you have written clearly about what you think that memory or experience did to shape your lifetime attitudes and beliefs about yourself and your self-esteem. Review what you wrote down about what a more productive belief and response would have been to that memory. Make sure you write down a more productive belief, even if the current belief has been useful in some way in your life.

So go ahead and do this project and prepare for day one. This is the longest project that you will be given, please spend the time it deserves on it. Finishing this project is going to illustrate to you how you got your self-esteem to where it is today and then the end of this project is the first day in the development and enhancement of your advancing self-esteem. Exciting eh?

Day One

All for one, one for all.
Alexandre Dumas, *Les Trois Mousquetaires* (1844)

We need balance or an awareness of balance to develop self-esteem. So, we need to have a bit of an assessment of how balanced your life is, as of today.

There are a number of essential topics for you to explore and just have an increased awareness. It is not intended to be too analytical, just to get you really aware of the place that you are at right now. So all you are required to do is make some notes and have a think about some of the following areas.

Firstly, what about your career? Write down what it is that you do to earn a living and what you think about your work. Do you work just to earn an income, or is your work your love, or are you somewhere in between? Are you pursuing any interests or any particular goals with your career? Do you have a long term career vision? Add some details about whether or not you are doing anything to develop your career. Are you delighted with your current career progression? Are you pleased with the career choices that you have made? Write it all down.

Secondly, how happy are you with your existing relationships? That can be friendships, partnerships, marriages or all of these. Does the quality of your relationships affect your life or your level of well-being? Do you think that the nature and quality of your relationships reflects the nature and quality of your life? Write down what sort of relationships you have and how they vary. Who are the people in your life that you are the closest to? Did you include yourself in any of those notes? Write down a bit about the relationship you have with yourself.

Thirdly, are you brimming over with health, vitality and energy? How do you currently feel physically? What are the reasons for that? What do you do to maintain your fitness? Do you feel well?

Fourthly, are you rolling in it? Or are you desperately trying to find a halfpenny to scratch your backside with? Or are you somewhere in between? What is your current financial situation? What do you think about money? Are you happy with the money you are currently earning? Do you save? Are you a big spender?

Next up, what are your goals and values? Both of these areas we look at in more detail later in this book, for now, we are just stock taking. What do you want from your time on this planet? What things or aspects of life are important to you? Are you currently doing anything to achieve your goals? What are the reasons that you do the things you do?

Do you invest in yourself? By that, I mean do you commit to your own personal development? Hey, you must have some interest in your own personal development as you have invested in this book about getting your mind more capable of enhancing self-esteem. Write down how else you invest in your own personal development.

What do you do to have fun? What makes you laugh? What hobbies do you have? What do you do to relax? What do you read? Are your hobbies things you do by yourself or are they with other people? Do you enjoy social interaction? If so, do you have enough of it?

These questions are just aimed at beginning to get your brain juices flowing and moving around in that head of yours. Having begun this initial explorative process by answering these questions, please now write down each of these following categories of life and give each category a percentage score as to how satisfied you are with that area of your life. Be as honest with yourself as you can be:

- Your immediate physical environment (surroundings and possessions).
- Your level of health and fitness.
- Your current career position.
- Your existing relationships.
- The level of romance in your life.
- Your own personal development.
- Your present financial situation.
- The fun, leisure and recreation that exists in your life.

Now then, it is time to recall those art classes or those technical drawing episodes from school, I am going to be very demanding here because I want you to draw a large circle and divide that circle into eight quadrants. Basically, that involves dividing the circle in half, then those halves in half and then those quarters in half. I did have to read that back a few times when writing that, but I feel quite pleased that I got that right first time, in fact I feel smug.

Anyway, now go ahead and label each of the eight spaces with each of the eight afore listed categories. Then, write in your percentage score of satisfaction and draw a line on that quadrant at the place where that percentage would be. So that you can be 'filling up' that quadrant with the level of your existing satisfaction in that category. The final thing to do in this tumultuous task is to then remove the outer, original circle.

Then, there it is, you have created your very own wheel of life that is representative of you. Now imagine that your carefully constructed wheel is on a bicycle taking you along the road of your life. Would it give you saddle sores delivered by a bumpy ride? Or would it be a nice smooth and balanced joy to ride? Notice the areas of your wheel of life that need attention and begin thinking about your immediate areas for improvement and development.

As we progress, if you do this exercise again at a later date, you may well find that developing in one area will often have a by-product, a knock-on effect of improving and developing other areas too. Investing more time and energy on your own personal development may well enhance your career and subsequently increase your income. If your romance is blooming and improving, then your relationships may well improve too and even your health and fitness!

The main aim of crafting your wheel of life is not to get each and every category to 100% because whatever our current level of satisfaction is, we get used to it sooner or later and just want more. For example, you may start off, as of today, being 80% happy with your current level of income but as you discover more of your own potential (as you are going to be doing), you may think that you are worthy of more and have the abilities to warrant more. Subsequently, your satisfaction may decrease temporarily. The aim here today is to get a snapshot of where you are at right now and get you heightening your awareness of yourself from day one.

Balance and Congruence

Before moving on to day two, I want to prepare you a bit for the reasons why these first two days are filled with investigation of yourself. A sure fire way to accelerate your mind's ability to believe in yourself and have the kind of self-esteem that you want is to have less or no internal conflict. That means that you want more balance and more congruence in your life.

I attended a large networking meeting last year with lots of varying types of people representing various types of companies and businesses. One of the speakers at this event was talking about and explaining how online networking had helped him go from redundancy to having his own lucrative business that he really enjoyed running, and that he had created this level of success in a relatively short period of time. While he was not exactly the greatest public speaker that I have seen, there was something about him that made me want to give him business and that made me like him. He was congruent, balanced and there was an air of honesty about him that I really warmed to.

What do I mean by congruent? Or balanced? I mean that this is a description of how you are when the things that you do, the things that you say, and the things that you sincerely believe in are all aligned. They are all pulling in the same direction. Have you ever met someone who said one thing and you know they meant another thing? I once worked in therapy with a lady who kept on telling me how happily married she was, but every time she said it, she played with her wedding ring in a manic way without realising what she was doing. She was demonstrating incongruence. This is an obvious example, I know, however, in order to attract and develop the right conditions in your life for increasing self-esteem, you want to have more congruence in your life.

Congruence and balance is a sort of deep-rooted honesty about who you are as an individual, and this congruence is attractive and appealing. What's more, it is attractive and appealing in your relationship with yourself as well as others thinking that way about you. People are powerfully attracted to congruent individuals and congruence attracts success which is wonderful for your self-esteem enhancement. When you experience more of what you consider to be success, your self-esteem increases. It works for you beyond the conscious awareness of most people so that you just get instinctive feelings about people who display congruence and are drawn to them without consciously knowing the reasons why.

Congruence is not only something that is about how others perceive you. As I said, it is also important in how you perceive yourself. If you want to make a powerful change in your life or if you want to feel better about being you and you really want particular things in life but keep on doing or getting something else, then incongruence will exist in your own perception of yourself too. This can create obstacles and barriers to you achieving increased self-esteem.

So how do you go about becoming congruent? Or having more balance? The first step is to think about what is written here in this day's learning, the second step is going to be to complete your project on day two. One of the aims of day two is to heighten your awareness of yourself to create far more congruence; which is going to serve as a wonderfully worthwhile foundation for your self-esteem.

One of the things you are going to be doing is figuring out your values; your values are what are important to you in life. Examples of your values include helping others, having security, enjoying freedom, continuous learning, experiencing love, having a family and so on. You may be aware of your values right away, and areas where you already have balance may start to present themselves more readily, while others may take some exploration. That is the aim of day two's project.

Also, as the lady with the wedding ring did not do; pay attention to your body. Is it giving the same messages that you are verbally giving? You shall be learning more about the physiology of self-esteem later.

Your body and your neurology have been organically developed over thousands and thousands of years to provide you with precise, accurate and real feedback about congruence and balance. If you are at a dinner party and you are smiling and chatting nicely and doing your best to be charming but all the time you are thinking 'I cannot stand these people' that uncomfortable feeling in your body and that thought in your mind is an incongruent signal, you lack balance and people will know that and sense it. When you experience a true and natural sense of peace, joy and

22

genuine balance, really truly enjoying the company of those people, then that is a sign that you are aligned and are moving in the right direction.

One of the most effective ways to experience more congruence is to do more of and engage more in the things that you love to do. Things that you enjoy. These things help to create congruence and that balances you.

When you do what you love, enjoying your life and then letting go of all the other stuff, you get to spend more and more time experiencing that sense of joy, contentment and happiness. These are the states of self-esteem. What's more, people really do like to be around someone who is doing what they love! That includes you being around yourself. You will love yourself a lot more when you are enjoying what you are doing when looking to achieve your enhanced self-esteem.

One of the things I love doing is running the various training courses that I run regularly. Things like my self-hypnosis seminars for example, are one of the most powerful approaches that I have encountered for helping people to live congruently and with balance. The self-hypnosis seminars put people in control of their own minds to let them move forward and create the kind of lives that bring them unlimited satisfaction and happiness. During those times, for me to then experience other people making powerfully progressive changes, getting in control of their minds and lives and to heighten their own experience of themselves, really does ensure that I then experience that sense of deep congruence and balance that comes from fully being myself.

The amazing power of congruence and balance existing beyond your conscious awareness works just as well for your own self-esteem targets. We can all think of examples of personal development goals that we want to achieve where the goal may include ideas relating to people, integrity, health or happiness, but where the subsequent actions and behaviours that you take just do not support the goal.

Alternatively, you may have encountered people that carry out and display behaviours that do match their actions. Those people are congruent, and that congruence and honest balance sends an unconscious message to people and to yourself, it sends a message to your own mind that says 'you can trust this person to do what they say' and this attribute is a bedrock of self-esteem. So forwards and onwards to day two whereby I want you to bear in mind that notion of creating congruence. Make sure you have created your wheel of life before moving on though.

Now then, as I said before, prepare to get very used to reading the words 'Project for today' as you are going to be reading them every day from here onwards.

Project for today: Design and create your own wheel of life and see how balanced your own life is or is not as of this very day. Discovering where you are at as of today is going to help you know where to move forwards to.

Day Two

Two lovely berries moulded on one stem;
So, with two seeming bodies, but one heart.
William Shakespeare, *A Midsummer Night's Dream*

Ahh, a fresh new day beckons and we move on to day two. Before you begin to get your mind into the kind of shape that sees it brimming over with self-esteem, in order for you to get the very most from this book, you now have a second and final day of discovery and research about yourself. Today really is going to be your own introduction to yourself.

Before we begin getting into all the wonderfully exciting techniques and strategies for allowing yourself to enhance your self-esteem, you are going to get some more information from yourself about yourself. The following are known as logical levels and arise out of the field of Neuro Linguistic Programming (NLP). The information from your previous day's project with the wheel of life should be revealing areas of your life that require some attention in order for your life to be more balanced; now I need you to tell *you* some deeper information about yourself in relation to those areas that you are identifying.

One of the main aims of this book is for you to achieve your personal best and develop your sense of self in your life. By having a personal sense of direction, resolving inner conflict and managing personal change, you can start spending much more of your life and your time in a state of balance, happiness and harmony; all brilliant for creating more self-esteem. When you spend more of your time in those kinds of states, you are at one with who you are – there is little or no conflict or stress within you. You are then best placed to begin to have increasing levels of self-esteem.

One of the aims of today is to clarify your thinking about yourself. Your success with this book is going to come from within you; once you have your mind balanced, and you enhance your

25

awareness of it, you are then in a position to manage things in the 'outside world', what I mean by that is the world outside of your mind. Once you have that inner awareness and balance, that 'outside world' starts to shape itself to fit with your inner awareness and emerging balance. So, once you allow your mind to be in the shape for developing and growing your self-esteem, your external world begins to fashion itself accordingly. Again, more exciting stuff, eh?

Your project for today is going to be to write at least paragraph about each of the following zones of your life. When I say at least a paragraph, I really do mean *at least*. The more time and energy you invest into this process, the more you will benefit from it.

Your Environment

This refers to everything 'outside' us. This is about where and when any of your self-esteem issues happen, or where and when there may be a problem.

Explore the environment of your life. Is your environment conducive to achieving enhanced self-esteem or solving any particular obstacles to that goal? This can include where you live, where you work and the people you associate with.

Write down exactly what your environment actually is. When you think about the current level of balance in your life, when you think about your own level of self-esteem and the success that you want to achieve, write about where and when you do the things or plan to do the things required to achieve that. What are the external influences on you and your life? What do your physical environment and your appearance tell the world about you?

Your Behaviour

Secondly, write and tell yourself exactly what you do, by that I mean write about your everyday behaviour. Think of your behaviour as the tip of the iceberg, the bit of you that can be seen by the world. Contrast that to all the things that are to follow; your purpose, identity, capabilities, beliefs, values; these are all internal thoughts and feelings.

Let me give you some examples of typical behaviours:

- Speaking what is on your mind.
- Getting angry easily.
- Managing your time well.
- Smiling regularly.
- Blushing when gaining eye contact with someone.
- Meeting new people in social circumstances.

It is very likely that you will have a characteristic pattern of behaviour that supports enhancing your self-esteem and a pattern of behaviour that can also hinder and obstruct having increased self-esteem. Think about how others might think you behave contrasted to your own thoughts. Identify your behaviours that you or your friends would say are typical of you. I know lots of my friends and close family would all say that I do not take anything seriously and that they think I tend to make jokes at inappropriate times!

If you have a particular problem in your life that you wish to deal with, your behaviour is sometimes about what the problem actually is. When writing about your behaviour consider and think about the following questions:

Is your behaviour, what you actually do, conducive to achieving your desired outcome of boosting your self-esteem? How do you behave? What do you actually do on a habitual basis? What do you do at specific times? Think about your actions, how you think and what you do. Then of course, make a note of what you would like to be characteristic of you.

Your Capabilities

Let yourself know what you are capable of and what you would like to be capable of. Your capabilities are the resources that you have available in the form of skills or your capabilities could refer to qualities, such as sensitivity, adaptability, flexibility and so on. When you begin to create some more balance in your mind, in your life and within yourself, you become more and more aware of how much more capable you are than maybe you had realised. Then you can discover how resourceful you can actually be and you can release the best of your abilities. This then propels your sense of self-worth.

Do you remember the 2001 Wimbledon tennis championships? Goran Ivanisevic was not considered to have any chance of doing well; at least his form in the build-up to the tournament had suggested such. However, his belief in his purpose and in himself allowed him to enter the tournament on a wild card. When you saw or read interviews with him during that tournament you could see that his passion was intense. He stated that his purpose was to give something to his country that had been devastated by conflict. Ivanisevic wanted to inspire his country and he did just that. When you watched him play, it was obvious that he played each and every point as if it were match point. He won the Wimbledon title in a final that I will never forget and that is recalled by many, myself included, as the best ever.

When exploring and writing about your capabilities, this is also about how you do certain things. How do you do what you do?

Do you have the capabilities to achieve your desired level of self-esteem or solve certain problems at the present moment in time that may be hampering your path to enhanced self-esteem? What are those capabilities that you have? What capabilities do you need to achieve this increased self-esteem? Do you need to do something or take some action to gain more capability to achieve your desired level of success? Think about mental skills, physical skills, your experiences and coping skills. What do other people think your capabilities and strengths are?

Your Beliefs and Values

Your beliefs and your values relate to the reasons why you do what you do; the reasons why you do the behaviours that you wrote about earlier. Our beliefs are views about ourselves, other people, the world and situations that we consider to be true. They are invariably emotionally held and not really based on fact, we are going to explore your beliefs some more later in the book, here are a couple of examples of what I mean by beliefs:

- I believe that no-one can be trusted.
- I believe that I do not deserve to be happy.
- I believe I can learn from the experiences of others.
- I believe that honesty is the key to a happy relationship.

Are your beliefs conducive to having enhanced self-esteem? For example, some people harbour the belief that 'Money is the root of all evil' when trying to be better off. Do you hold negative beliefs about yourself in relation to your self-esteem that hold you back from increasing it? Think about what your beliefs give you permission to do in your life.

Think about what you value in life. Ask yourself just what is important to you in life; what drives you to be who you are? What motivates you to be the way you are? Your beliefs are driven by your values and it is your values, which determine how you make decisions throughout your life. Values are qualities that you hold to be important to you in the way you lead your life. You may value these things for example:

- Honesty.
- Openness.
- Integrity.
- Fun.
- Learning.

One way you can find out what you value is to identify something you really want; so go ahead and think of something that you really want. Now ask yourself this question; what will that give me that I wouldn't otherwise have?

When you have subsequently answered that question to yourself, ask it again.

Ask yourself; what do I want? An example response might be: To reduce my weight.

Then you ask: What will that give me that I would not otherwise have? The answer might be: A body I can feel comfortable showing off.

Then ask again: What will that give me that I would not otherwise have? The answer may well be: Freedom.

To get the most from this exercise, you need to take the question as far as you can until you get the simplest answer and the question can be asked no more. When you go as far as you can, you end up with a core value: what it is that is really important to you. In this example it was freedom. So here you are establishing what your values are in life.

We all have our own interpretation of what these values mean and how we know they are met. It is important not only to have values but also to know how you will recognise that they are being satisfied. When writing down what your values and beliefs are about yourself in relation to your desired levels of self-esteem, do be honest with yourself. Think about the reasons that you made certain decisions today and yesterday and throughout your life. What factors led you to make those decisions? What beliefs and values would you like to have or do you think you need to have in order for you to create more self-esteem for yourself in your life?

Your Identity

This is about asking who you are. This is about you getting an idea and feel of your sense of self. This kind of investigation can go on for months and years to really pinpoint, so go easy on yourself here. What roles do you currently fill in your life? What roles would you like to fill in your life?

Ask yourself who you are. Is there a metaphor or character that sums up your identity? When I started training to be a therapist, I used to think of myself as a knight in shining armour! Is your identity suitable in helping you achieve your desired goal? What is your identity and how do you identify yourself to the world and how does that relate to the notion of having more self-esteem? Think about who you are and your feeling of purpose being who you are.

Your identity creates your own sense of self and what you consider your identity to be may well contain statements describing how you think about yourself as a person, statements such as:

- I am a successful person.
- I am an optimist.
- I am a shy person.
- I am an easy going person.

Remember that when you think of these statements about yourself, you can sometimes close down the opportunity to be anything else, so be careful when noticing what statements you use to describe your identity.

These are the things that you believe make you who you are. Begin to think of your mission ready for the next level. I work with so many people and companies that have big dreams and visions of how and who they want to be and so very few of them seem to know how to achieve those things, so I made it a mission of mine many years ago to 'help more and more people of the world to achieve their dreams' and this is one specific mission of mine. I have other missions and visions that last temporarily too.

Your Life Purpose

This is sometimes interpreted as being very spiritual, that may or may not suit you. Although your life purpose can have a spiritual connotation, what I would like it to refer to here are the larger systems of which you are a part; the grander scheme of things rather than the specifics of your life. Understanding more about your own sense of purpose means understanding (or at the very least exploring), the relationships between us and the larger systems which we are a part of. So when thinking about your purpose, explore some of the larger systems of your life, these might include:

- Your family and friends.
- Your marriage or primary relationship.
- Your community.
- Your company or organisation.
- Your faith.
- Your world.

It is this sense of purpose that exists most profoundly beneath the conscious awareness of most people. Beneath their immediate awareness is where most people make decisions about you as to whether you are someone they want to be in a relationship with, marry, conduct business with and so on; like when you get a 'gut feeling' about someone.

In his brilliant book *Seven Habits of Highly Effective People*, Stephen Covey refers to having a sense of purpose as being your legacy. Your legacy does not have to only refer to what you leave when you die; what do you want to leave when you leave a room? When you leave a company? What would you like to leave when you leave a relationship? What would you like people to think

31

when you leave a meeting? That is also your legacy and thus can become your purpose.

Your purpose is lived out by the kind of person you are.

What has been your main purpose in life so far? What purpose are you on this earth in this life for? If there was one main purpose what would it be? Does it support your desired levels of self-esteem? Think of your personal missions and work missions for example and think of what you might like your life purpose to be and let yourself know that. There may be several, if so, put them in some sort of order. Think about your purpose, your mission and your vision. I am going to discuss this in more depth later in this book; it will be useful for you to contrast what you write now with what you discover later.

By becoming aware of your thinking at each of these levels and writing it down you are beginning to influence the process of personal balance and creating the foundations for a mindset of self-esteem and confidence. You need a fertile land upon which to plant your seeds. By working your way through the questions at each of the levels and exploring each of these levels from the stance of who you are today, you begin to develop some balance and congruence and be far more aware of yourself. This is crucial for you to fully benefit from the rest of this book and the techniques, strategies and insights contained therein.

The more thorough you are and the more you give yourself to work with, the more you will benefit from this book.

Project for today: Write at least a paragraph about yourself on each of the logical levels.

Day Three

If the triangles were to make a God they would give him three sides.

Charles-Louis Montesquieu, *Lettres Persanes* (1721)

Today is an easy day in contrast to the previous two days of exploration. When you think about having self-esteem in whatever way is right for you, please have a think about what outcomes you want to occur. This is our topic for today. One of the fundamental and most basic aspects of self-esteem development is the idea of having well formed outcomes in your life. What's more, I am going to be placing a large emphasis on them at several stages throughout this book as it is so very important to your own self-esteem. You see, you get whatever it is you focus on the most.

Well formed outcomes are very well documented these days, but so very few people actually do use them, and even fewer people create them properly and in a way that is useful for developing self-esteem.

Having well-formed outcomes for your life can create wellbeing in business, your personal life, in relationships and so many more of the areas that you want to have more self-esteem in. This includes growing our sense of self. So please be as flexible as you possibly can be while learning this; and I do not mean absorbing this information while doing the splits! It is important in boosting your brain and developing the mindset for self-esteem that you have the best possible formed outcomes for you in your life.

I use well-formed outcomes in business and individual interactions. I was speaking at the National Exhibition Centre in Birmingham in the United Kingdom earlier this year and I used well-formed outcomes for how that event was going to go for me, as I do with every speaking engagement I have. The evening prior to the event, when in my hotel room, I imagined myself delivering my material professionally and being delightfully entertaining at the same time. I imagined that my audience experienced a wide variety of emotions while watching me and were connected with me throughout the time I was on stage. I also imagined the sound of rapturous applause when I finished. Of course, I was much more detailed than this brief example and of course, there was much rapturous applause that following day.

As the first three projects that you have been asked to do have been quite full-on, I am going to go easy on you today in preparation for some of the more demanding days that lie ahead. Before I give you today's project, I want to give you some information and guidelines for what I mean by the term well-formed outcomes:

As of now, today, this very moment and for the rest of your life, I want your goal-setting to become more than just plain old goal-setting. You want to go beyond that and step into the realms of desired outcome development. You are making your future more desirable, more alluring and more sexy. Hey, if you do not want your future to be sexy, that is OK by me, you do this in the way that appeals to you, it just so happens that I like to think of my future as sexy and sometimes I wrongly assume that everyone does, enough rambling. So, you are going beyond setting goals and moving into the realms of setting outcomes.

As you think about any area of your life that you would like to update or change or plan better for (or make more sexy), or if you have an unfulfilled dream or something you are working towards, then creating a well-formed outcome can begin to get your unconscious mind and its related processes driving you towards that, without you even having to know how.

Now, I have mentioned that I want you to think in terms of outcomes instead of goals, however, goals do have their place in your plans and we will be working on the goal achievement for more self-esteem later, for now though, focus on outcomes. How are goals and outcomes different from one another? Put simply, goals are general and outcomes are specific. An outcome represents a goal that has been made more specific and precise that then enables you to have a very clear understanding of what to do to achieve it.

When you have a head filled with wonderful well-formed outcomes, you enable yourself to create specific images, sounds, feelings, internal dialogues and words. Then that vision with its sounds, sensations and other ingredients that combine to create that outcome stimulates your abilities and resources for achieving that outcome. The outcome should be stated positively in terms of what you want: as you are going to be reading about much more later; the human mind does not directly process a negative. I explain this in more detail later.

It is desirable, and something I am going to insist upon in later days, to have your outcome described in sensory based language: In terms of sights, sounds and sensations; what will you see, hear and feel with that outcome? See how we are forming the outcome, crafting it? Think about the kind of outcome you want from reading this book. Think about how you will be when you have a deep rooted growing belief in yourself. Create outcomes for these things in your mind and allow your mind to guide you in that direction.

Also, ensure that the outcome is created by you and it is in your own control. You need to make sure that you install that idea in your mind that your enhanced self-esteem is something that is not reliant on others in any way. Changing others directly lies outside of our control.

The vast majority of people and companies that I encounter and work with operate in a stimulus/response mode. In his wonderful best selling book *The Psychology of Persuasion*, Kevin Hogan talks about this in great detail and it is there that I first read about this topic. This stimulus/response mode is where something happens and you respond. Something else happens and you respond. So, as of today, instead of continually reacting to the various stimuli in your daily life, creating desired outcomes is about looking at how to control your own life instead. Having good, progressive well-formed outcomes in your mind allows you to decide what you want and shows you how to achieve it. As I have described already, having well-formed outcomes is having the ability to imagine the precise outcome of a process before beginning that process. Establish an idea of what your life is going to be like when you have increased self-esteem.

World-class athletes from all over the world use well-formed outcomes to achieve top performance in their field. The best golfers visualise a shot before they hit the ball, the best football players imagine scoring a goal before it happens. There was that story (could be an urban myth) about the guy who was incarcerated for years in a prison and had mentally practiced his golf shots inside and when he came out he was a brilliant golfer.

You, in relation to the amount of self-esteem that you want to have in your life, want to heighten your awareness of that successful outcome before it occurs.

Knowing the outcome in advance is exceptionally powerful. So go and begin to design your future, make them as sensory rich as possible. Create it and allow your unconscious mind to deliver the results.

Pretty easy going day today, eh?

Project for today: Get relaxed, breathe comfortably, and take some time out to really imagine several of the outcomes of your life that will be undeniably convincing to you that you have achieved some success in boosting your self-esteem.

Day Four

One for sorrow; two for mirth; three for a wedding; four for a birth.

Mid Nineteenth Century Proverb

OK, so the song went something like this:

Happy talking, talking, happy talk, talk about the things you'd like to do, you've got to have a dream, if you don't have a dream, how you gonna make a dream come true?

How very prophetic Captain Sensible was being in the 1980s with his pop hit. So, you have to have a dream.

One of the amazing gifts that we have as people is the desire to have dreams of a better life and dreams of success. In addition, we have the amazing gift of possessing the ability to establish goals to live out those dreams. If that was not enough for you, what is even more amazing is that we have also been given the ability to not only dream but to pursue those dreams and not only to pursue them, but the ability to actually set goals and make plans to achieve those dreams. Isn't it amazing to be a human being? To have that within our own control, is that not amazing?

Now you may be thinking that I am going all soppy here and I know that even though it is in your own control, sometimes people hold themselves back for one reason or another and that is where this book comes in.

I did most of my Christmas shopping this year online. Some may think me lazy, but I love to shop that way. The convenience of not having to scrap at the 'bunfight corral' with all the other frenzied shoppers really does appeal to me. Throughout my experiences as an online shopper, it has dawned on me that setting and achieving goals really is as simple a process as placing an order. Therefore, when you now complete each of the following steps in this ordering process, it becomes a bit like ordering your goals!

Before you run through the process of setting and working towards your goals, it is important to know what they are and what you want. How can you achieve if you do not know what it is you really want? So many of us want something different from our lives but do not really know what we want. How do you find out what it is you want in life?

Some time ago now, a lady came to see me and she had successfully stopped smoking with me and as she had enjoyed the success after 30 years of trying and failing to stop smoking, she was so happy that she felt capable of doing anything. She brought in what looked like a shopping list of things in her life that she wanted to change!

At about the same time I also got an email from someone that receives my regular ezine, and they wanted all sorts of different things to happen in their life, and could not decide what to focus on. I want to give you some pointers on helping yourself to know how to know what you want. Does that sound a bit confusing? OK, let me put that more simply; how to know what you want.

In the 1990s, and during most of the time I have ever been employed, I was doing jobs that I found to be unsatisfactory or that I simply did not enjoy. When I first began to invest in myself and I took my first personal development study course and learnt some of the main aspects of the personal development fields that I wanted to work in, I was amazed by the resources that already existed within me. As I learnt more about the various modern psychological technologies that I have come to love so much, two questions became more and more insightful to me. Those two questions were (and still are):

'What do you want?' and 'How will you know you have got it?'

As these two very powerful questions came up more and more, I realised I had not applied them to myself as I should have done. What did I want? The more I asked myself that question, the less I knew the answer. However, I was sure of the fact that I did not want to remain an employee for anyone and I certainly did not want to keep on doing what I was then unhappily doing. I also knew that the personal development fields I was discovering, that were resonating so well with me and helping me so much, were to be at the heart of my future in one way or another.

So, as you stop and think with regards to your own life, maybe a specific aspect of it, or of your life as a whole (not a hole!) have a good think and identify anything that is currently part of your life that you would rather be free of or something that you wish you could let go of. Really think about that.

Almost everyone has examples of one sort or another. What about these ideas:

- A current job you may well not enjoy.
- Anything that represents a barrier to your increased self-esteem.
- Unwanted habits that cause you problems or unhappiness.
- You may be unable to spend time doing things that make you happy.
- Being stuck in a dissatisfying or limiting relationship.
- You may have a limiting belief about yourself that does not serve you well.

Take a few moments and figure out what you no longer wish to have in your life, the things that if you were free of would help you to enhance your self-esteem. I spend a lot of my time ranting to people and companies about stopping focusing on the past. You will experience my thoughts on that throughout my work; I really do not like traditional ideas of focusing upon or languishing in the past. I believe in focusing on progressive and positive things. So when thinking about things that you want to let go of or be free of, remember not to focus on these things too heavily, just know what they are for now.

Following my own initial discovery of certain fields of personal development and the things I learnt within that discovery, I progressed to studying hypnotherapy, NLP, emotional intelligence and many more fields of interest to me. I went on courses all over the world, read hundreds of books, listened to audio programmes on hundreds of topics, I trained in all sorts of other therapies too. My current consulting rooms would have no space left on the wall for all the pieces of paper I own that have official certification written on them if I decided to put them all up (I have so many letters that I am entitled to put after my name that it would look like I was writing the alphabet; it is ridiculous). You know what though, even after all that study, all that behaving like a training and seminar junkie, I still was unsure about what direction I really wanted to go in. I did know what I did not want and I also knew what sort of direction I wanted to go in, and so I handed in my notice at work!

I knew that I wanted to have lots more time to satiate my need for knowledge and furthering my studies, I knew that I wanted to have financial freedom and that I wanted to be doing work that fulfilled me and helped others. Establishing within my mind more of an idea of what I wanted in life began to heighten my sense of self more than I had ever experienced. I knew that I wanted to continue having lots of opportunity to be mischievous, have lots of fun, lots of excitement and adventure and that I wanted to be happy and wonderfully peaceful in myself. As of today, you have the benefit of someone else telling you how that happened to them so you do not have to embark on the same lengthy process, instead, you can follow the same steps in a far, far shorter period of time.

So, once you have identified the things that you would love to let go of or move away from in your life, the next step to take is to identify anything that is part of your life that you definitely want to continue in the future. The things that you know continue to allow you to feel good about being you.

You all have good things in our lives; everyone does. Some of you may not think so, but you do. Identify those aspects of your life you definitely choose to continue to have. They can include things like a good level of fitness, intimate friendships or relationships, your own home, any feelings of satisfaction, a loving family or your current income. Although I will focus on it in more detail later, reminding yourself of all the good things in your life is crucial to developing self-esteem.

Then, once you have listed some (or all) of the wonderful things in your life you wish to continue, you can now list anything and everything that you would like to be part of your life in the future. Think about what you want to have or to be in your life in the future. When you thought about your well-formed outcomes yesterday, what did you envision to be an integral part of your life that you actually already have now?

If you have sometimes had difficulty knowing what you wanted in the past, it can be good to choose big-scale things rather than small specific things. Think about what it is that you definitely want in your life in the future, no matter what. What will exist in your life when you have more and more self-esteem? This may include a loving relationship, a better income, fulfilling work, intimate friendships, personal development and enhancement, to be free of your unwanted habits, good quality health and fitness, a sense of real happiness and other wonderful feelings. You know, I just refuse to live without my regular dosage of bliss and want that to continue to happen.

These are examples of the big scale things. Next, you can begin to become more specific about them, however, be careful not to over specify, by that I mean if you want to have fulfilling work, but you don't know what you want to do, get specific about what has to happen for your work to be fulfilling, for example; working with people, being outside in the fresh air, making a difference in the world, able to study new things and so on depending on whatever 'fulfilling' means to you. Remember to think about what fulfilling really means to you and not just think about the examples that I have given here; that may not really be what you truly find to be fulfilling.

It is not necessary to be specific about what that work would necessarily be. Just set your target as 'fulfilling work', and then ask yourself how you will know you have got it. Then you are going to follow the powerful goal setting and achievement process coming up to let your unconscious mind work it's magic for you. Hurrah.

So, you can see and begin to get a handle on what it is that you really want and once you know that, you can begin to work towards how to get that. We are building the foundations for increased self-esteem without actually focusing on it too much just yet.

Project for today: Think about your dreams and your goals in relation to your self-esteem. What would you like to achieve when you have more self-esteem? What other goals do you have? What is important for you to do in life? For each goal, write out the answers to these questions in as much detail as you can:

- What do you want?
- Can you describe it more precisely? If so, then do so.

- What exactly will you see, hear and feel when you achieve this?
- Approximately how long do you think will it take to achieve?
- When do you want to achieve this goal? (Now? Next week? Next Year?)
- How will you know that you have achieved your goal? (What will prove to you that you have achieved it?)
- How will you measure your progress and how often will you measure your progress in working towards this goal?
- What resources will you require to achieve this goal?
- What resources do you already possess to achieve this goal?
- Where will you find the resources you need?
- How will your wheel of life balance be affected when you achieve this goal?

Day Five

Alone and warming his five wits,
The white owl in the belfry sits.
Lord Alfred Tennyson, *The Owl* (1830)

Welcome to the fifth day, I do not have five gold rings for you today as the song goes, but my goal for today and tomorrow is for you to have a thorough and foolproof system to set up your self-esteem related goals and a plan for achieving them. We are talking goals from here onwards, or as the wonderfully enthusiastic Brazillian football commentators would say:

'GOOOOOOOAAAAAAAAAL!'

Whatever time of year it is that you happen to be reading this book, have a think about the festive period and the excesses that are associated with it and then think about what you are like at New Year. You know what it is like at New Year, people often make pledges to themselves and others of things they resolve to do. Suppose I have set myself a goal to reduce my weight by 3 kilograms during the month of January. Let me bring your attention back to my previous discussion from yesterday when I mentioned being able to order your goals in just the same way as I did my online shopping.

I compare the online DVD store to life's amazing virtual goal delivery system and am delighted to say that if you follow these steps, your self-esteem goals are in the bag.

The First Step: Decide what you want

You will already have begun this process as of the previous day's project. To help you to be sure of your goals, take some quality time out for yourself to be quiet. This is something that hardly any of us do enough of in our busy lives. We tend to manically rush, and we are constantly paying attention to the noise that is going on around us. Your heart and mind really do enjoy times of quiet, to look deep within. It is when we take the time to do this that our hearts are set free to soar and take flight on the wings of our own dreams and goals.

Think about what really thrills you. When you are quiet, think about those things that really get your blood moving. What would you *love* to do, either for fun or for enhancing the quality of your life? When you have a wonderfully enhanced sense of self what would you love to accomplish? What would you do if you were guaranteed to succeed? What big thoughts move your heart into a state of excitement and joy? When you answer these questions you will feel great and start becoming aware of what your goals are and of course what they should be.

Life is too short to not pursue your dreams. Someday your life will near its end and all you will be able to do is look backwards. You can reflect with joy or regret. Those who dream, who set goals and act on them to live out their dreams are those who live lives of joy and have a sense of peace when they near the end of their lives. They have finished well, for themselves and for their families.

So, once again let me get back to the online goal ordering system; I cannot and do not expect the online DVD company to send me a film or comedy show before I have actually sent them my request, neither should you expect life to supply the resources to create wealth, make more sales, stop smoking, reduce weight, lower stress levels or be filled with self-esteem. So, choose the outcome that you require as per one of our previous days learnings, so that now it can be ordered.

In order to do this, ensure that you get a vivid, sensory rich idea on how you want it to be; decide upon what it is that you really want and then make sure that you do really state it in the positive. For example 'I want to achieve and maintain the size shape and weight that pleases me' is infinitely better than 'I do not want to eat too much' because you want to focus on what you want and not what you don't want. Be sure not to state the goal of 'I want to lose some weight' either. You people; the readers and followers of my work are certainly not 'losers!'

Your unconscious mind treats negative and positive in the same way when it learns. Positive and negative thoughts are not processed by your neurology in the same way that they are when you say them, for example; If I were to now say to you 'Don't think of a pink elephant' it is a command that is very difficult to actually do. In order not to do it, you have to do it! When someone says 'I don't want to be lacking in confidence' you have to imagine lacking confidence to understand the sentence! You are dominating your mind with the thoughts of the things you do not want.

The Second Step: Get your goal in writing; make it real and tangible

Before I can place an order for any DVDs, I have to find the right order page for the DVD I want to buy. However, before I can find the right order page, I have to type the right key terms into the search bar. I would not find the right order page if I do not use the right terms. Wouldn't it be madness for me to type '**not** the first Star Wars film and **not** the second Star Wars film . . .' or to have typed in 'I do not really want anything with Jack Nicholson in it . . .' in my search for the DVDs I did want? (by the way I love Jack Nicholson). Write what you do want, and be as specific and particular as you can. Therefore I type in 'Star Wars Episode III : Revenge of the Sith'. This is the DVD I want to locate and buy.

As I have already mentioned, it is a common thing for people to think about what they want out of life in negative terms. They talk about 'getting out of debt' when they really mean that they want to experience 'financial security and freedom'.

Your unconscious mind, your very powerful brain is going to deliver precisely what you order. Vague orders bring about vague results and we never see the connection between our requests and what shows up. Too often we place careless orders unknowingly, and then wonder why things do not turn out the way we wanted them to. Focusing on 'debt' brings a constant supply of it into your life, even if you are trying to get rid of it. After all, it's like putting 'not debt' into the search tool. You're not looking for the 'debt' order page, so stop using that expression today! I liken doing that to driving towards a lamppost and thinking to yourself 'I really do not want to hit that lamppost'. When wanting more self-esteem to be ordered, you want to focus on boosting that.

Commit to the goal that you have by putting it in writing. It is like entering it in an imaginary search box. It is also the fastest way to get to the right order page. One more thing: write it in present tense as though it is already happening. Make it happen in the now.

So, maybe your goal statement in writing will be something like, '30 January 2006: I have now reduced my weight by 3kgs'. Getting it in writing automatically takes you to life's 'order page' but you are not done yet. The DVD is not on its way until you have completed the order all the way to the end of the process.

The Third Step: Loading up your shopping cart

Now, if you are going to invest your own endeavour in doing something, you need to have a good reason, so let yourself know exactly what the reasons are that you want to achieve this goal. What is having enhanced self-esteem going to get for you? How does it benefit you? What then becomes possible for you? Allow yourself to really explore all the benefits that you are going to get from achieving your goal. The more you do this, the easier it is to be enthusiastic and motivated about it, and then of course the more your self-esteem enhancement is simply inevitable.

In my DVD purchasing experience, after I typed in 'Star Wars Episode III : Revenge of the Sith' into the website search engine, it presented me with a list of 'Star Wars' DVDs. Some were the earlier films. After carefully selecting my specific choice, I clicked 'add to shopping cart'. This is a logical step; after all, I cannot really expect the online DVD people to despatch the DVD until I have advised them which one in particular I am after.

This step is comparable to the step of adding detail and sensory information to your goal statement. You need to spend time creating a more detailed description of the thing you desire. Instead of '30 January 2006: I have now reduced my weight by 3kgs' you write, '30 January 2006: I am delighted and proud now that I have made really powerful steps to achieving and maintaining the size, shape and weight that pleases me, by successfully reducing my weight by 3kgs. I am truly happy at how easily this was achieved and am grateful to myself for having successfully completed this. I am now developing a more progressive relationship with myself and expect to reduce more weight with more ease this following month too.'

Following this step means that you have just added your desired goal and successful outcome to the 'special life shopping cart'.

The Fourth Step: Where are you? Give your shipping address

Now that the DVD is in my shopping cart, I have to tell the DVD company where to send it. This step is the part that ensures that my ordered DVD is distributed to my location. This now brings together two key pieces of information into one virtual place. Without this step, the DVD people cannot send me the DVD because they have no address for the package.

Goal setting is no different. Just as the DVD and my address had to merge into one database, the goal you want needs to be merged with your personal information also. Notice that during this step, it is not the actual DVD that came together with my actual home; it is simply a representation of the DVD that came together with a representation of my home.

The same needs to happen with a representation of the thing you want, and a representation of you. How? You must imagine yourself achieving that goal; being that ideal weight for example. It might take a few minutes to really generate the images in a vivid way. Nevertheless, with the power of disciplined thoughts, you merge the thing you want, with the person you are. Your mind is the virtual database where it all must come together before life can fulfil that order. This is similar to the well-formed outcomes exercise we did before; that was preparing your mind.

As you think about your goal now, having it in the positive form, vividly imagine just what you are going to see, hear and feel when you get what you want. As you are doing that, turn the brightness and colours up in your imagination, make the sounds louder, even add some of your favourite music or other wonderful sounds and turn up the wonderful feelings that go with it, think about where in your body those feelings are going to be when you achieve that goal and really make them more intense.

Then *believe* in that which you want. As you imagine that goal, view it and perceive it like you just know it is going to happen, in the same way that you know if you drop your cup of tea, it will fall to the floor. You just know it will happen. The same way that you know the sun is going to rise tomorrow, fair enough I may not see much of it here in England, but I just know it is going to rise. View your goal and that which you want through the same lens; that you just know it is going to happen. So every time you think of your goal and the sensory rich outcome, think of it like you just know it is going to happen. Have I stressed that point enough? Have I repeated that enough times for you? As you imagine seeing the version of you with more self-esteem, just know that it is going to happen.

Then, as discussed earlier, think about how you will know when you have achieved that goal. How will you know? Remind yourself.

I once had a client whose main goal was to be wealthy. I asked her exactly how she would know when she was officially wealthy and she said that she would have more money. So I asked her if she thought that if I gave her a fifty pence piece, would that make her officially wealthy? 'Of course not' was her reply. 'More money' did not turn out to be specific enough evidence for her having achieved her goal, so we went into the detail of what she would see, hear and feel when she was officially wealthy. So get your own brain sure that it knows exactly what to work towards.

The Fifth Step: Receive confirmation of your order

After I filled in my shipping address, it asked for my credit card info. This is where I pay for what I want.

In setting a healthy weight goal, to 'pay' traditionally refers to 'dieting', 'pounding the treadmill' and so on. But that is not what I mean here.

So what is the price you pay? Well, it is not an easy price to pay. But it is easier than 'paying' with unreasonable, unrealistic diets and fitness regimes. To take the final step in the order process, to do the last thing required before you receive the order confirmation, is to allow yourself to experience the feelings you feel when the goal is achieved. It is easier said than done, but you need to take your imagination exercise just one step further; let me give you an example:

You are out at a social summer event with friends, wearing that new dress or that favourite pair of trousers, huge grin on your face, you can smell the air and it smells sweet, you feel a sense of freedom in your tummy as you move your body and you can see your friends expressions on their faces looking at you excitedly. As you meet some friends that you have not seen for a while, they tell you how amazing you look to have reduced your weight. You look over at your proud partner and you whisper to them 'I did it! It has been tough at times, but I did it! Let's really enjoy ourselves today!' And your partner says 'You really did do it, I am so proud of you and what you have done.'

This is your price. Ensure that you get into your imagination and associate with your results. Do not watch yourself doing it; you did that in the earlier steps, now it is time to *be* you doing it. It is like if I asked you to imagine watching yourself flying around in a roller coaster, the imagined experience is far more intense if you imagine actually being on that roller coaster and experiencing it from the point of view of actually being on it rather than imagining watching yourself being on it.

Now, if you really do spend some time generating those kinds of images and thoughts in your mind, and feel the excitement and enjoy the gratitude for the success then you are there! You have paid for your goal. Then as those feelings develop and enhance inside of you; that is your confirmation. Trust yourself and your unconscious mind to keep its promise, and go about your life in peace. No need for desperate measures; you have already paid the price. Go about your life with a calm assurance that it is already done. Then go about your goal sensibly. The results are on their way and will connect with you in a natural way as you go about your day-to-day activities. Simply follow the thought. Think about new behaviours that you will need in order to have more self-esteem (lots more of which are coming up in this book) and begin to generate them.

The Sixth Step: Expect success to arrive, and be ready to let it in

After my bill was paid, and I received my order confirmation, the DVD was on its way. I needed only to expect it, wait for it, look out for it, refrain from cancelling it, and answer the door when it arrived.

One very powerful thing to do here is to now let go of your goal. Detach from the outcome.

When you really, really want a specific outcome or really, really want a particular dream, your system sometimes tenses up, and it becomes increasingly hard to achieve it. The more you grip tightly on to it, the more you strangle it and suffocate it. Instead, find a way to become relaxed with the notion of not getting it. This maintains a sense of relaxation and acceptance while you are moving towards your goal. Imagine your goal as an actual 'thing' and imagine letting go of it, cut the ties that bind it to you and let it happen unconsciously without you having to continuously engage in conscious thought processes about it.

As for your (hypothetic) goal to reduce your weight by 3kgs by the end of January, if you have gone through the entire order process, and you have received confirmation, all you must do is expect it, look out for it, refrain from cancelling it with unbelief, and when opportunity knocks (because it will), simply answer the door.

So finally: **The Seventh Step:** Celebrate your successes!

People need to celebrate more, so celebrate your successes. Not just the big goal, but every milestone along the way. If you want to slim down, celebrate every few pounds lost (with something that supports you, like new clothing, not chocolates). If you want to be a healthy non-smoker, celebrate your first day smoke-free, then your first week, first month and so on. If you want to be wealthier, celebrate reaching certain levels of wealth – celebration sends a strong sense that you are doing the right thing to your neurology and makes it easier and more enjoyable to continue replicating your success.

When you have set goals for your self-esteem to develop, celebrate you doing things differently for a week. Celebrate being able to do some things that could not do before. Even celebrate having felt consistently good about yourself for a period of time.

Project for today: Run through this entire process for your most important goal; to have greater self-esteem. Aim to use this process for as many of your goals as you can in the future.

Day Six

For in six days the lord made heaven and earth,
the sea and all that in them is.

Exodus ch. 20 v.11, The Bible

When we are happy it is far, far easier to enhance self-esteem. Happiness is something that is a highly individual and subjective state, a complex combination of physical, mental and of course emotional elements. For some people, it is lazily lying on a sun lounger on holiday without a care in the world. For others, it is having their intelligence stretched by studying and being stimulated intellectually. For others like myself, it is the moment after they have completed a marathon; I was overjoyed the moment I stepped over that finishing line for the first time, that feeling lasted for a few days and I can still tap into it when I remember and vividly recall it. Happiness can last a fleeting moment or it can last several days or weeks. For some, depending on how they go about defining it, happiness can last for an entire lifetime.

I have worked with CEOs of massive corporations, millionaires, celebrities and sports stars and it has been my own personal experience that happiness is not necessarily dependent on events, levels of success, or our achievements. In fact, so much research, examination and discussion from the fields of modern personal development has shown us that happiness results from *how we process our experience* rather than what our 'real-world' experience actually is.

As I mentioned, from my own experience of having worked with many people that are considered wealthy and successful, I have encountered many, many of these people that are also desperately unhappy. Our own personal interpretation of what happiness is does not necessarily equate to what our external circumstances are, or with our levels of wealth or success for example.

So, to define it further still; being happy is a process. It is a process that involves selecting. Out of all the information and experience that is available to you, you pay full attention to what gives you most rather than what gives you least. Let me illustrate what I mean by that by taking a look at two people with very different ways of dealing with the events of their lives.

Arthur had worked in the conveyance team in the same solicitors firm for many years. In fact, he was the longest serving member within this department and was considered by many of his clients and those from within his profession to be very good at what he did. He was not an ambitious man, far from it; he had stayed at the same level of responsibility where he felt comfortable, and had seen many colleagues, and many partners from within the firm come and go. He had a long memory which helped the detailed legal work he did. However it did also work against him at times, because whenever Arthur talked about his work and his role within the firm, the aspects of it that he seemed to remember most clearly were times when he had been taken advantage of, taken for granted or treated poorly. His friends and family had heard lots and lots of stories about such things. Arthur complained, believed himself to be undervalued and even felt cheated; but never once did he express it or say anything directly and neither did he take any action where and when he felt badly treated.

Alice had experienced a relatively hard life in many peoples opinion. She had raised eight children on just her husband's small and irregular income as a handy man and what she could claim in benefits. Only now, in their latter years, were they in a position to relax. Although they had not saved a penny and only lived on a state pension, they were happy. When one of her grandsons asked about her life one day, Alice said in an instant that she had been very, very lucky; she had had the best kind of husband a woman could have, wonderful children, and a roof over her head with lots of friends all around her. Yes, it had been hard at times, but she would not have swapped it for anything else.

As you can see, Arthur and Alice had very different ways of processing their experiences. Arthur had been relatively successful at his work, but somehow what stayed with him was not the fact that he had been a valued member of his firm for forty years, but the incidents in which he had felt neglected or taken advantage of. Out of all of the aspects of his working life that he could have remembered, those were the ones that stuck in the forefront of his mind. He was rarely contented, though in fact he actually did have numerous things in his life that could have made him so – if he had been aware of them and noticed them more readily. Alice had a head filled with memories that could easily have made her think and believe that life had treated her poorly; she could have felt hard done by very easily; but she naturally focused on the things that had made her feel valued, supported and content. She was someone who had a knack of being happy.

Is Happiness a Choice?

These two people are very representative of so many individuals that I work with that obviously process their experience of life in very contrasting manners. As a consultant, I encounter a number of key issues that consistently arise with people that I work with and I want to go into each of these areas in more detail.

We all respond to challenges in a variety of ways. How do you respond to a challenging situation?

When Arthur felt taken advantage of, made fun of or neglected, he just kept his feelings to himself, he wallowed in his anger and resentment like a hippo wallows in mud, and then allowed it to fester inside of him. In some cases he bottled this stuff up for years. Subsequently, from his continual dissatisfying experiences, he developed a generalised belief about people at his work place and in life that 'you're only noticed if you're loud and outgoing'.

I reckon that Alice could have felt justified in being resentful or bitter too. Her life had been filled with poverty and struggle, but her attitude was that it was pointless (like a broken pencil!) to go on complaining about it. She would blooming well speak her mind if she felt angry, and those that knew her knew this well! However, she downright refused to allow those feelings to linger. So Alice had made a very different generalisation about life. That's right, she thought it was great on the whole, she had a lot of fun in life and believed that anything could be resolved if you wanted it to and were prepared to work at it. Alice believed that there was no value what so ever in getting worked up about things that you could not change so she did not do so for any great period of time.

So as of this very day, I recommend that you act on and let go of things that bother or annoy you; laugh about them if you can, giggle about them, refuse to take them seriously. If there is nothing that you can do, stop going over and over the events in your mind and stop telling others incessantly about them; telling others is just the same as continually telling yourself.

Every time you repeat something you embed it further into your own mind. Choose to ingrain good experiences. If you find a person, a circumstance or a situation continues to make you unhappy, dissatisfied, angry or uncomfortable (or any other emotion that you consider negative or undesirable), find a way to change it. Slamming the door shut right in the face of experiences that limit you is the way forward.

OK, if a negative thought creeps into your mind and you do not want to be carrying it around, or you are worried that it could spread into a full blown unpleasant feeling (oh-no!) run yourself through this procedure as often as possible:

Firstly, if and when naughty old negative thoughts enter your mind in any form (that may be an image, your internal dialogue, or just a feeling) that support any slightest idea about lacking self-esteem in any way at all, then first of all you need to stop the thought from spreading. Shout the word 'stop' to the thought in your mind to stop it from spreading. You may want to say or shout it out aloud instead of in your mind, but the people in your immediate periphery may think you unusual. This stops it from spreading any further.

Secondly, take two or three deep breaths from the area beneath your tummy button. Some really good deep breaths and alter your physiology so that you are standing, sitting or holding your body differently than you were previously. Move your body to a different stance or position. Move the position of your arms or legs; get into a different position physically than you were when you had the negative thought or feeling.

Thirdly, and here is the interesting bit, imagine making the thought into a 'thing' and put the thought (the thing) on to a screen of any sort. We need to dispose of that thought. So, imagine that you have a cinema screen or a picture frame or one of those good old etch-a-sketch screens in your mind and you are putting that old, negative thought on to it. Go ahead and just put it on to a screen to dissociate yourself from it. This stops it from becoming a seed in your mind and growing into a full blown unpleasant state of mind. Then send that screen away, banish it, make it smaller, smash it, 'white' it out, just get rid of it in any way. Banish that thought from your mind. Remember before remote control, old TVs that used to have the knobs on the outside? When I say 'white it out' just imagine that you are turning the brightness up full and whiting out the entire negative thought. Just get rid of it and be in control of your own mind.

This is the start of you being in tune with yourself and really learning how to tune into you is at the heart of you determining your own levels of self-esteem and owning your own life. Getting properly tuned into yourself is what creates the experience of congruence, where you are doing, wanting and being the same thing in harmony and with balance. Tuning into yourself involves you now being aware of your experience of life and giving that experience the respect it warrants and deserves. It means that as of today you give yourself the right to own your experience of life and act on it accordingly.

Our friend Arthur did not own his experience of life and that is a real shame, even more so because there are so many people like Arthur. He suppressed his negative feelings and so became unbalanced and incongruent. These buried feelings that he refused to notice then sparked off his continually negative internal dialogue whereby he went on remarking and complaining to himself for a long period of time afterwards. Neither had Arthur learnt how to fully appreciate and enjoy the things that did actually go well in his life. Alice verbally expressed what was on her mind and then she carried on with her life. She spent most of her life focused on the present and the future, where she had the capability to control and influence things, rather than on the past, which had already gone and cannot be changed.

So also today, I want you to begin to fully acknowledge your feelings, really be aware of what your own experience is more of the time.

As of today, it is also vitally important for you to begin to become aware of how you interpret your every day experience of life. When you notice how you translate your experiences it shows you exactly how you create your own internal 'realities'. Let me explain what I mean by that. Every single moment of every single day we are bombarded with information from all of our senses.

We experience a multitude of colours, sounds, sights, sensations, feelings and in addition to the immediate sensory information, we also have beliefs, opinions, thoughts and attitudes. We have communications of various means and this list could go on. On so many levels we are taking on masses of information. The vast majority of it is beyond our conscious awareness and this is a good job; if you had to be consciously aware of everything you would go mad! There is just too much.

How do we deal with this? One of the ways that we have adapted to dealing with the overload of the vast array of information that comes to us from internal and external experience is to *simplify and generalise*: you can see that Alice's generalisation about life was an empowering one. Compare this to Arthur's generalisation that just added to his resentment and bitterness. It was his belief that people deceived and undervalued him; that was also his expectation. Arthur just got into that groove, he then just carried on noticing everything that made him miserable and unhappy instead of making the most of what could well have given him happiness and pleasure. You see, when you generalise in a certain way, it alters how you judge your own level of success too.

Whose life was a success here? You or I cannot answer that, only Alice and Arthur can answer for themselves, success only exists in your own mind. Who do you think generated the most belief in themselves and had the best level of self-esteem? I think we all know. So if we look again at Alice, who in contrast, believed there were some things that were beyond her power to change about her life, she never once attempted to kid herself that hard labour, poverty and irregular income were enjoyable to experience, however, she did have the ability to gain enjoyment and meaning out of the choices she could make; the things that she could do something about. Alice was quite rightly proud of being a good mum, she was proud of always feeding her family and keeping her children adequately clothed. Her home was welcoming. She was dependable, considerate and caring and in return received loyalty from friends and family who all enjoyed being with her.

So, also for today, think about and examine what generalisations you are making about people, life and the world. Really notice how what you believe invariably tends to 'come true'. One of my favourite quotes from my friend and teacher Jon Atkinson-

Garside is 'what you believe to be the truth is the truth for you'. Very interesting and thought provoking.

As you think about how you interpret your experience of life, think about what other information you might be overlooking. In particular, listen to your internal dialogue; recognise what it is that you say to yourself on regular basis? Your internal dialogue both reflects and confirms the generalisations that you make in life. How about this for example, have you ever caught yourself saying in your own mind 'that is typical'? If so, go ahead and catch yourself doing it and then ask yourself 'typical of what?' Of who? How is it typical? If what you are noticing is negative, look for some exceptions that defy your negative statement. The way you think and communicate with yourself on a regular basis each and every day sets the frame for how you will feel and behave in the future. Remember, your internal unconscious mind is a rich and fertile land that will provide a wonderful home for any and all seeds that are sown regardless of whether they are negative or positive, so if you continue to sow the wrong kind of seeds in the form of negative thoughts, negative generalisations and persistent negative internal dialogue, what kind of feelings and results do you think are going to grow within you?

Finally for today, I want you to create some space inside your mind to notice and pick up on certain evidence that may run against any negative generalisations that you ever have or discover. A great way to do this is to get into the mental routine of breaking down negative thoughts by adding the magic word 'and' at the end of any negative statement and then follow it up with something which is also true but neutral or positive.

Let me give an example of that 'I have had a terrible day at work. **And** my wife is still happy to see me' or 'no one had time for my feelings today. **And** I shall make time for myself this evening.' Using 'and' in this way both allows you to say what you feel and helps you dismantle your old, negative generalisation. In time, the continual process will eradicate the negative stuff happening in the first place. This requires some diligence and practice, so really be on your guard more of the time and do not just let old habits or patterns take control of your mind, you have a mind of your own, stretch yourself and be in charge of it.

Project for today: Take some time to relax and be comfortable somewhere. Tune into how your day has been and think about any aspects of it that you may have considered negative and make a statement about it. Then, add 'and' to that statement to neutralise it as described at the end of today's learning. Get into the habit of doing this every day and then as best as you can, do it all the time.

Day Seven

We've been waiting seven hundred years, you can have the seven minutes.

Michael Collins (1890–1922)

If I asked you what it was that you noticed about your day today, what would you tell me? Arthur and Alice went about their lives noticing very different things, like people viewing the world through differently tinted spectacles, I know you have all met someone that you could describe as wearing 'rose-tinted spectacles' when they look at a certain thing. I know I can be described as wearing them whenever I watch my football team Nottingham Forest play football, I always think they play better than they are and get more involved with the games as they are the team I love and support.

When Arthur noticed something that upset him, he immediately linked it to a long line of other things that had upset him in the past, so he reinforced and strengthened them. Alice was really good at noticing simple and smaller things and made the most of little delights like her garden flowers blooming in the spring, or hearing a joke one of her children had heard at school. She always noticed humour, fun and kindness in other people and in fact began to be drawn to these qualities when she met it; this was as a result of noticing these things so prominently. On the seemingly rare occasions that something did upset her, she treated it as an exception or an unusual isolated incident that had occurred in her world, she certainly did not allow it to confirm a negative view. This way, it is easier to let go of negativity if and when it occurs.

Beginning today, I want you to practice honing in on and focusing on what is enjoyable in your daily life, focus on aspects that make you happy and what is fun or fulfilling and satisfying about yourself, your life and other people. Observe people who you know are or think are contented and especially people who

59

are optimistic. I would even recommend that you ask them about how they do it and then replicate those instructions yourself. Find out what it is that they pay attention to. Often, it is a lot easier to find something small to enjoy and really focus in on.

Then, at the end of each day, spend a few valuable minutes 'mining for gold' by making a list of all the good, the wonderful and the pleasant things that happened during that day. This is so very good for your self-esteem. Even if it was 'only' a smile that you received from the postman, recover it, enjoy it again and re-experience it. This way, you continue to end each day on a positive and progressive note. At the same time, you are now building into your mentality a wonderful new habit of noticing what is good in life. Even though this is not your project for today, really consider taking some time each day to note all the good things that have happened.

A little while ago I caught two grown adults spitting on a sports car that was parked outside a shop. I asked them why they did it and they were very open in saying that they did not like people that obviously showed off wealth. Hmm? They just saw this as a negative statement; they viewed it with contempt and resentment. Would you want to carry that around inside of you every time you saw a sports car? Would they not be far, far happier if they wished the owner well because they are doing well? This perplexes me and I cannot imagine these people being genuinely happy in their lives if they hang on to resentment towards others for something as ridiculous as owning a sports car. Incidentally, the sports car was mine.

It is just like whereby Arthur continued to complain that the trains were getting more and more unreliable nowadays, Alice told her husband how a young man in the waiting queue at the supermarket had let her go in front of him as she only had two items to buy. She was often delighted by things like this. Arthur's sense of letdown meant that he would notice, instead, how someone pushed ahead of him to grab a taxi. The contrast in the colour of the glass in life's spectacles that you choose to wear makes a big difference

Do you have stories of your life? Do you tell stories about the fun elements of your life? I want you to get into that habit of retelling good and uplifting stories, and refraining from telling bad ones to yourself and others.

You know what, Arthur owned his house and his car and enjoyed a week away skiing every winter and had an exotic holiday each summer, he was also a fully paid up member of the golf club (is that a good thing?) and had a nice healthy pension fund, but despite all this, as I said earlier, he really did not own his life. Alice owned and enjoyed hers.

So today, make a list of things in your life that you could feel satisfied with. Read it through to yourself. If you still feel discontented, ask yourself what you really want. Take your answer seriously, then make sure that you have well-formed outcomes for what you really do want in your life.

Think about what it would be like in the future to make a comprehensive list of all the things in your life that you really should be happy about. What would it be like to read it regularly and add to it, then remember more of its contents and you progress through life and look for more and more aspects of each and every day that you can add to that list?

We are drawing to a close as far as Arthur and Alice are concerned; we have fresh pastures to move on to after today. Ask yourself if you think that you are like Arthur and are less than satisfied with life or unable to find the happiness in it. Or maybe there are times when you feel that you could identify with Arthur's experience as you verge on having this temperament yourself at times?

Before you then begin that process of being more aware of those times and changing how you filter your experience of your life, it is undoubtedly going to help to know more about how you structure your experience of happiness. To work this out, you want to find out how you actually go about being happy or unhappy.

Project for today: Take two pieces of paper: on one, jot down as much information as you can about the last time you were happy, and on the other, write down information about the last time you were unhappy. For each, consider the following questions, I have given some sample answers to help:

- What was each occasion like? Explain the sensations that you felt and what your experience actually was.

- How did you know you were happy and/or unhappy? What did you see, hear, feel, taste and smell with each experience?
- Did you know straight away, or was it later when you looked back on it, that you knew you were happy or unhappy?
- What made you happy? What was the cause of your unhappiness?
- What was occurring all around you with each experience?
- Did you have any internal dialogue during either experience? What were you saying to yourself before, during and after each occasion?

Look at the patterns that emerge within your answers and examine the information that you have just gleaned, because this is valuable stuff. I tend to process the majority of my own experience visually and kinaesthetically. Feeling miserable is a very particular feeling, and when someone is miserable, they often add critical internal dialogue too. Knowing this is not going to change external events or stop things from happening externally, but it can help you to respond differently and more agreeably.

For example, you could modify the tone of your internal dialogue and make the content more encouraging (for example, by reminding yourself of how you succeeded in a particular way before). I can remember when I was researching for an article once, I had to go to the library to pick up a book and I found myself whining to myself about not wanting to go, I was telling myself in an antagonising tone that I had far more important things to do and to get on with. I was effectively talking myself out of going and doing what I had to do. So I thought about the sexiest voice I could think of; Marilyn Monroe.

I imagined Marilyn, sexily, huskily humming into my ear that I was going to enjoy going to the library and I am telling you that things began to change inside my brain. Then I imagined two of them whispering seductively into each ear that I was going to go to the library and I smiled and went about my merry way. Lots of people ask me how it is that I manage to drive myself to get up in the mornings to go running before the working day begins, often in the wind, rain and darkness. I tell them that when I awake, I have gospel choirs singing 'hallelujah' in my head and brass bands thumping out a roaring tune and I remind myself of images inside my head of how wonderful it is to feel fit and to cross the line at another race.

We can use our internal dialogue so very much more than we do.

To condense it down, for you to be happy, all you need to do are these three things:

- Firstly, refuse to put up with anything that makes you unhappy by doing something about it and changing it.
- Secondly, discover all the things, or as many of the things as you can that make you happy and do them more and more.
- Thirdly, teach your brain to filter your experience of life so that you pay close attention to all the things that you enjoy and that enrich your day-to-day existence.

Happiness is one of my favourite ways to be, I like it less than I enjoy experiencing bliss and ecstasy, but it is still a wonderful way to be. Happiness is a way of processing experiences and it is a direct result of what we pay attention to. You know what; it is such an easy-to-produce state which relates very specifically to you as a unique individual.

Discovering just what happiness means for you is an essential step to experiencing more and more of it. So many people spend a great deal of time thinking 'I just want to be happy', and to those people I say, continue to ask yourself those poignant questions: What does happiness mean as far as you are concerned? How would you know if you were happy? What would your experience of happiness be?

I would like happiness to be something that from this day forwards you can actively create, amplify and manage, because you have a mind of your own and can use it to establish and create the attitude of mind which encourages more happiness. At the same time, it is a by-product of how you are going about managing your life and the way you perceive things in general, this has a huge impact on your levels of increased self-esteem which we are going to be focusing on in much more detail very soon.

As I have been explaining, happiness often involves making a positive generalisation from a specific experience instead of a negative one. I always used to think that happiness is our own unique experience, however, you do not have to limit yourself to just your own flavour of happiness. Think about friends, family and colleagues that you know for sure are happy and ask yourself; how do they do that? Observe people that you do not know who seem to be happy; what is it that you notice about them? How did you conclude that they were happy? Model these people's flavours of happiness to enhance and develop your own repertoire. You will be increasingly happier more of the time, when you take control of how you actually do the process of being happy.

Day Eight

Pieces of eight, pieces of eight, pieces of eight!
Treasure Island (1883) ch. 10

If you have been diligently following each day's learning, the processes and doing your daily projects, you will be getting to know yourself a lot, lot better by now. Now before we go any further, I want to talk to you about Kermit the Frog and Miss Piggy.

I know, I know, bear with me, there is a very valid reason for this.

If you were a real pig, how would you go about getting handsome, celebrity frogs to fall in love with you? When I read a book by Kevin Hogan and Mary Lee Lebay called *Irresistible Attraction* I realised how.

Take a look at Miss Piggy from the Muppets. She was always very outgoing and confident, but more importantly she had amazing self-esteem. She thought and firmly believed that she was stunningly beautiful and she displayed it in a very dramatic way. Everyone fell for it, everyone found her to be glamorous. What's more, Kermit the frog even went and fell in love with her! But let's look at the truth of the matter – she was a pig!

Now she was no curvaceous Jessica Rabbit from the film 'Who Framed Roger Rabbit' who was a text book stunner! Miss Piggy certainly did not have the qualities of your typical super-model; I would even put my neck on the line and say that she was a bit chunky! I could be receiving a karate chop if Miss Piggy catches up with me!

Developing self-esteem and oozing confidence can and does distinctly increase your ability to be irresistibly attractive and to attract success. It can and very often does create an illusion or aura of value, worth and desirability.

Why do we find a person with high self-esteem to be attractive? What is it about them that draws our attention and admiration? Is it the mystique? Is it an aura? That certain *je ne sais quoi*?

Look at what is happening here; a person who exhibits strong self-esteem is telling the world they value themselves. So when a person recognises their own self-worth and exhibits that to the rest of us, we start to think that they know something that we don't! In other words, they think they are special and have value.

Likewise when someone shows the world that they have low self-esteem, we tend to believe and think that if they do not think very highly of themselves, then why should we be impressed or respectful of them? We certainly don't usually allow ourselves to be dazzled by them.

In both cases, we simply go along with the estimation that what the person has signalled to us is valid. We tend to just believe the verdict that the person has put upon themselves.

So why is that attractive? We, as humans, are naturally attracted to that which has been deemed valuable. We also tend to want to be a part of a larger group. We often follow the lead, join groups, and go along with the majority opinion – just to be part of the group.

Even if we are not Brad Pitt or Angelina Jolie or we do not have the face that warrants going on the cover of glossy magazines, having self-esteem is attractive and being more attractive enhances our success in many, many ways. When you feel good about yourself, others feel good about you. So that is what is next in our plan; to get you feeling good about yourself. You are then more ready than ever to welcome success into your life.

Self-esteem is the way that you feel about yourself, self-confidence is the way you feel about your abilities. Both can enhance your ability to attract partners, pay-rises, friends, sales, success, achievement and lots more. I think it would be valuable to learn how to increase your own self-esteem today. Hey, if it gets Miss Piggy pulling at someone's (some-frogs) heart strings, it can do the same for you.

Today we are getting right into the heart of our main subject matter: Self-esteem.

Self-esteem is incredibly important. In fact, I think it is so important that I am going to say that again. Self-esteem is incredibly important. Even if you think that you have lots of it already, you can always benefit from more. Lots of people have the notion that it is the same as self-confidence; however it is far more than just self-confidence.

The word esteem itself literally means 'to put a value on'. As you might have noticed and connected in your mind, the word esteem shares the same root as the word 'estimate'. Therefore, we can see that self-esteem, really does just mean the value we put on ourselves.

When someone has a high level of self-esteem, they have a genuine, deep rooted sense of self; a really good relationship with themselves, they actually like (and often love) themselves; they are consistently aware of and well in control of their thoughts, beliefs, behaviours and their overall internal state; and they have a sound sense of purpose, or rather they act and behave with purpose. These qualities and traits are not magical gifts that we were dealt out at birth, oh no. One of the key concepts in many of the world's self-improvement or change programmes or writings is the idea that you can learn to do anything that anybody else does.

So that is where we are going to start today, by indicating and illustrating just what it is that people with highly developed self-esteem actually do, I am going to break it down into easily understandable portions so that you can replicate them and apply them to your own life straight away today.

Being Aware of Who You Are

So very many of the individuals that I have worked with over the years tell me that they lack self-confidence. I hear individuals say it and other individuals demonstrate it so very often. As I mentioned earlier, self-esteem is the value you place on yourself whereas self-confidence relates to your confidence in your abilities. Confidence refers to trusting in yourself; at its root, the notion of confidence means some kind of action that is to be undertaken in some way. Your confidence usually relates to your own ability to carry something out or to undertake a task or simply to have some kind of level of competency. Your level of confidence (or lack of it) is something that is inherent in your ability to do something, to behave in a particular way in a particular situation, to take on a particular challenge.

It has been my experience (and will no doubt seem obvious when stated) that it is almost impossible to be confident in yourself if you do not have a solid foundation of self-esteem in the first place.

I have a great friend and although I am naturally quite biased, she has always been very gifted in her particular field and was a legal secretary. She studies law in her spare time and is very diligent and thoughtful about her work. She completed her initial training and joined a very reputable local legal firm. In an instant she was noticed for the high standard of her work and subsequently recognised by the senior partners as being intelligent, conscientious and diligent as well as very hard working. They firmly believed that she was an asset to the company and also noticed that she got on very well with her colleagues despite the often pressurised nature of her role. This naturally led to her being offered a more senior role at the end of her first year of employment for this company, and this entailed her having some additional responsibility along with an increase in her salary.

Following three seemingly enjoyable years in this role, the legal team office manager role became available and as she had been as good as running the office anyway, one of the company's most prominent and senior partners recommended to her personally that she apply for this vacancy. Despite the partner feeling that she deserved the role, my dear friend was rather perplexed and shocked by this suggestion; amazingly, she did not feel qualified, experienced or competent enough to take the role on or to even consider making an application. Over the years, rather strangely, she had always managed to successfully find reasons for dismissing praise, she told herself that she simply did not deserve it and that anyone could have done what she did and that there would come a day that one of the partners would realise that she was not that good at her job and she would be shown for what she really was. Therefore, she just did not apply. I found this remarkable and I still do. What's more, I know that you know someone just like this.

I encounter so many people like this. So many. These are the kind of people that have this low self-esteem and low self-worth and are therefore unable to generalise from the obvious successful results that they are having; even if others are telling them or they consistently receive acknowledgement of how well they are doing. It seems crazy. It is almost as if these people choose not to hear the praise and recognition that they are given. Because of this, my good friend that I mentioned earlier lacked the confidence to apply for that promotion (at least until I got my hands on her!) and many people with low self-esteem consistently and continually underachieve in their lives. The majority of them subsequently spend their entire lifetimes underestimating themselves and under-valuing themselves.

So today, what we are going to do is to explore what people with self-esteem actually do. Thanks to lots of research and investigation of those people that do have good levels of self-esteem, we are able to discover how they actually think and behave and by finding out how they do what they do, you can learn how to do it too.

When I worked at the Independent National newspaper in central London when I was younger, the newspaper had been bought by a new owner and was moving from where the previous owners, the Mirror group were based, in Canary Wharf in Docklands, London, to new premises in a slightly different part of London. A girl called Samantha was the Managing Director's PA and rather than using a proper project manager of some sort, the MD organised the relocation himself with Samantha's help.

She liked being who she was, had done well at school, this was only her second job and she had worked up the secretarial ranks to become the MD's PA. She did not mind being asked to help with anything out of the ordinary or unusual. The day before the office relocation was due to happen, the MD was involved in a car accident and had to take some time off due to being in hospital for a night and then off for a period of recovery due to the 'whiplash' he had incurred. One of the other directors then asked Samantha if she would oversee this relocation as she had been so involved in the process. She was very slightly apprehensive but of course agreed with almost no hesitation: after all, she knew most of the arrangements that had been made, and what's more the MD had a mobile that she could call if she was desperate.

Now I mention this because you can see the differences between the two people in my chosen examples. You see, Samantha had a more easygoing nature and attitude than the friend I mentioned in my first example, she was also far more at ease with herself, had a more defined sense of self and of course that naturally meant that she could take the challenge on that was required of her to take on the extra last minute responsibility when required to do so.

These two women were very capable; it is just that one had a low sense of self-worth, whereas one really believed in herself.

Project for today: Write down your answers to these questions:

- When you make a mistake, how do you tend to respond?
- On average, when you look at yourself in the mirror what do you tell yourself and believe you see?
- How do you react if your wants and needs are different from those of others around you?
- If and when you make a commitment to yourself, do you stick to it?
- How do you often react to what other people say about you?
- How easy is it for you to make eye contact?
- If given a compliment, do you accept it straight away, without dismissing it, diverting your attention from it or having to go over it in your mind to authenticate it? Expand your answer and explain it.
- Can you make a list of 10 things that you like about yourself without hesitation, just doing it straight away? Be sure to write them all down of course.
- What is your physical and psychological response when you are asked to try something that you have not done before, something new? Fully explain how you feel and expand on your answers.
- What internal dialogue do you use and what words do you say to yourself inside your own head when you are about to do something challenging or something that you consider to be difficult?

Really take some time writing down your answers; as always, it is good to see this kind of information in writing as well as it floating around in your mind without structure. Then, write down what your answers suggest about your relationship with yourself? How much do you like yourself? Are you kind towards yourself? Are you happy being you? Are you critical about yourself? Write these down because, as I have said before, you can then compare and contrast your answers when you have finished following these techniques and strategies. Tomorrow we move on to those strategies and techniques.

Day Nine

Pease Porridge hot,
Pease porridge cold,
Pease porridge in the pot,
Nine days old.

Newest Christmas Box (c. 1797)

As you look over your answers and responses to yesterday's project, I want to begin today with some of the best strategies to enhancing self-esteem based on the kind of questions I was asking yesterday. Let's dash through a few of those questions and then get stuck into some wonderful techniques and strategies.

How about that question from yesterday; when you make a mistake, how do you tend to respond? It is pretty usual and human not to actually enjoy making mistakes, you know that don't you? That is why we often feel embarrassed, or we sometimes deny their existence, maybe sometimes we even go as far as to blame others for our errors. We believe that the best way is to admit your mistakes, learn from them and take corrective action. After all, a mistake is a mistake – no more, no less.

On average, when you look at yourself in the mirror what do you tell yourself and believe you see? We live in a society that emphasises glamour and sex appeal. That is why most of us strive to achieve external beauty, but so very often we lose our uniqueness in the process. If we can accept the things that we would like to change without being unnecessarily hard on ourselves, we have then moved a very long way towards self-acceptance.

How do you react if your wants and needs are different from those of others around you? Your wants, needs and self-worth are as important as those of anyone else. However, that does not mean others will automatically respect them. As with Arthur earlier on, if you silence your own voice, others will not know what you want or need. It is up to you to claim your needs as important and learn how to respectfully assert yourself. With practice, you'll be amazed at how this will become second nature.

If and when you make a commitment to yourself, do you stick to it? If you have ever heard the phrase, 'my word is my bond', you will understand why honouring commitments is an aspect of healthy self-esteem. A commitment is a pledge and a pledge is a guarantee. When you make a commitment to yourself or others you are putting your integrity on the line. As you learn to demonstrate that you can be counted on to do what you say, you build your self-esteem and your credibility at the same time. That way, you and others will know that 'you walk your talk'.

How do you react to what other people say about you? When you put more weight on your own judgement than on others' it is easier to keep their words in perspective without becoming defensive. Your strong sense of self-worth allows you to maintain your power and still hear what others have to say without feeling bad about yourself.

How easy is it for you to make eye contact? When you meet people it is a good idea to think about how you make eye contact. It is one of the first things people use to form an impression of you. There are many myths and interpretations about what direct eye contact, or a lack of it means. The point here is that when you are interacting with others, they want to know the two of you have some connection. Direct eye contact is a great way to create a climate of harmony in any relationship and demonstrate your self-worth at the same time.

I was running a training course for a company a couple of years ago and a girl in the group who was one of the top performers would go bright red every time I mentioned her achievements or if I said anything complimentary to her. Some people really do find it unusual or difficult to accept compliments. This is going to sound very obvious; however, the simplest way to accept a compliment is to easily say 'thank you'. That does not sound too difficult, does it?

Use your brain to recall and remember compliments that you have been paid. Even if you think they are small or minor, remember one such compliment right now: imagine hearing it in your ears again, those nice words and then play it over and over or even better, say it out loud to yourself and then say 'thank you'. You can also experiment with a variety of voices and use a voice of someone that you find to be exceptionally encouraging or use a voice instead of your usual internal dialogue that seems the most natural and easiest to respond to.

It is important that you push your boundaries out here and really do this. Practice over and over the process of giving yourself compliments or remembering compliments that others have given you. What then subsequently happens is that on the next occasion that someone gives you a compliment (because by the end of this book you will be getting lots regularly); notice how you respond. Notice what your response was and regardless of how you responded, just offer a 'thank you' anyway. Your brain learns this new response as you keep doing it and then begins doing it instinctively and intuitively without you having to think about it.

When I asked the young lady about her getting embarrassed every time I complimented her, she responded as so very many people do. She told me that she felt she was nothing special and that at some stage everyone would realise. Hmmm. OK, so ask yourself if there is anything that you are afraid of people finding out about you. If so, find out exactly what it is that you do not want other people to know. Really ask yourself that and answer it thoroughly and precisely. The majority of people just do not want other people to think badly of them or to think badly of their abilities. This kind of worry or fear almost always has to do with what you anticipate happening and not what actually does happen; it has no real foundation, worrying about something that you think might happen is nothing short of madness. OK, I need to calm down; I am branding my readers as being mad. Surely you can see that anyone who worries about others thinking badly of them for no reason is anticipating the worst and is far more likely to encourage that outcome.

So today begins the reality check. The people that often undervalue themselves or believe themselves to be unworthy about their capabilities in any aspect of their personal or professional lives are plainly and simply underestimating themselves. Observe the people at your work or in your life that seem at ease and contented with themselves and notice that contentment and ability are just not related. They are not correlated. There are people who are far less talented than others that are at ease with themselves and their own abilities, you know there are. There are two very powerful questions, another two of my favourite questions in fact, that can help to unearth any other possible reasons for anyone's unnecessary worries:

- What stops you (feeling good about yourself)?
- What would happen if you did (feel good about yourself)?

You know what I am going to ask don't you? Write down your answers to these questions.

Now then, as you have it out and are scribing away, use your self-esteem journal (or that tatty piece of paper) to write on again. As we touched on earlier, I would like you to list anything and everything you can possibly think of that you like about yourself. It might be the way your teeth stick out when you smile, your child-like sense of humour, that you are kind, have neat hand-writing, can run a mile without throwing up or that you are honest. Absolutely anything applies here. It is important now to keep on collecting and adding to this list, make it an ongoing process that you continually add to this list whenever you think of something else. Then keep this list somewhere important to be able to refer to and remind yourself of its contents. There is so much to like about you!

The Times They Are a Changin'

Yesterday I asked you about how you feel when faced with challenges and new things. I can safely report that lots of us react with alarm, dread and anxiety when confronted with the prospect of a new thing! 'Oh, no, a new thing!' So if you do respond that way, today is going to be one of the seldom occasions that I suggest you write down the worst case scenario that you may have in your mind. If you take the right amount of time to really spell them out and write them down it will help.

Of course, much of the time this is enough to make you realise that they are actually ridiculous fears and also help you to realise that they are extremely unlikely. I bet they are. However, if on a rare occasion your worst case scenario could happen, think about how you would overcome it and what course of action would resolve it. You can even take it a step further still and think about someone you know would overcome it, think about what exactly they would do. How would they go about it? So, as of today, instead of letting any old fears fester deep within you as if you were bottling them up, choose to take them on and find healthy strategies for resolving them. Much more often than not, this approach is going to dissolve any sign of anxiety. However, if it does not resolve it, then your intuition and instincts may well be right: then simply do not do that thing!

Who Said That?

I have written a lot already about our internal dialogue, if you really have too much of it and you want to use it far better, I would recommend you read my best-selling book *The Secrets of Self-Hypnosis: Harnessing the Power of Your Unconscious Mind* as it has got a lot of information with regards to your internal communication. OK, I digress. The point I want to firmly establish here is that if you insist on continually telling yourself *not* to make a fool of yourself in front of others, or reminding yourself how things went wrong the last time, or indicating to yourself how useless you think you are, then that internal dialogue is well and truly amplifying your problem. It really is!

Imagine how you would feel if I were to use the same language that you use to yourself, and speak it to someone you love. So if I were to put someone down or be critical to them, I reckon that would irritate or annoy you and you may well jump to the defence of that loved one. Then why allow yourself to talk to you like that?

Instead, today, begin to think about what you would say to someone else in the same situation if you wanted to encourage them? How would you encourage a loved one? What language and tone of voice would you use? Write it all down and repeat it to yourself inside your mind to become your new, progressive internal dialogue. How do you encourage others? Use this way of encouraging others on yourself. Say those things to yourself instead of all that other nonsense that you may have persisted in saying. Ensure that you are convincing and sincere, make sure that you really mean what it is that you are saying. When you then communicate with yourself in that way, notice how that makes you feel? Notice what it is like to have that kind of progressive internal dialogue instead. It can be like a breath of fresh air for your brain because you are now nurturing it. As a result of engaging in it so very much, each time you create some internal dialogue, if you are more and more supportive, this makes a real difference to your self-esteem and your self-confidence and in turn builds a stronger foundation for your success.

Project for today: Write down how you would encourage a loved one to feel really good about themselves. Then repeat that encouragement in the same language and tone to yourself using your own internal dialogue. Allow yourself to relax and deliver this dialogue to yourself for 15–30 minutes.

Day Ten

My strength is as the strength of ten,
Because my heart is pure.

Sir *Galahad* (1842)

I am often asked if I can tell if someone has self-esteem. It is my belief that it is relatively easy to tell, though not many people actually notice the telling signals. One of the major indicators is that people with good levels of self-esteem just do not need to prove themselves. By that I mean that they do not need to:

- Brag or talk big.
- Put others down.
- Put on a show of themselves.
- Name-drop.
- Shine a spotlight on themselves.
- Tell you all about themselves and their own achievements.

It is often individuals who do these seemingly confident behaviours on the outside that actually have quite low self-esteem.

Last year, I was speaking at a large conference in Las Vegas and over 500 people were there to listen to the team of speakers of which I was one. The main organiser of the event was someone I had heard of and is very well known throughout their specific field and they introduced all the speakers on to the stage. I wanted to speak to them as much as I could and glean some tips or just get to know them and benefit from having this golden opportunity to meet them. In fact, I wanted to do the same with all the speakers and as we were waiting to go on stage, I took some time out to chat with all the speakers and they were all nice and at ease, no-one displaying any signs of anxiety at the prospect of speaking to this large audience.

However, I really did notice that the well known organiser asked no questions of any of the others, in fact they did not show any interest in any of the other speakers at all. This surprised me a lot. Even though the person had an outwardly relaxed demeanour and stance, the focus was always them. It was very much a one way conversation and centred entirely on them. I suspected that this person was not at all comfortable being this well-known organiser of the event. I confirmed this later on when that person asked me if I would spend some time with them to help coach them through some confidence related public speaking skills.

People with genuine, sincere self-esteem and a real sense of self, regardless of how well known they are, tend to display some very different characteristics:

- They have a quiet confidence.
- They do not fish for compliments, but they do accept them well: they know what they are worth.
- They may be quite humble.
- They recognise and are often interested in other people and their achievements.
- They may not be bothered about receiving external recognition.

You can detect from someone's body language if they have self-esteem or not as it usually speaks for them; it is like a huge antenna that tells you they are at ease with themselves. You will notice that they tend to be physically relaxed, standing up straight and tall, calm and precise in movement, they are decisive and without hesitation and they are comfortable making good eye contact.

You can see it for yourself in your world that despite there being so many people out there who display apparent confidence and ability, many may well actually doubt themselves and their own abilities (hey, you or someone you know may well be one of them). I know this very well as I spent years and years showing off due to a lack of self-esteem. Bear that in mind when you meet other people; whether they are dominating and outgoing or just quietly efficient, they may both have a serious lack of self-esteem or lack of belief in themselves.

Think about how you hold your body when you feel good. Think about the fact that mind and body are one single system and are very much related. When you hold your body in a certain way, your mind triggers related responses. So learn how to hold your body when you feel good about yourself and hold it that way more and more often.

Stop and think about people you know who have a strong sense of self: how do they behave? How do they seem to think? What is important to them? What do they believe? What tells you that they are genuinely comfortable with themselves? Trust your intuition here and make the most of your observations. Write your answers to these questions down as fully as you can.

Imagine that you were someone else that is watching you from the outside. As you look at yourself, how could you begin to incorporate what you have learnt from your earlier self evaluation and apply that which you learnt to yourself? Really have a think about that and make some additions to your notes accordingly.

Turning Up Your Self-Esteem

Now we are turning up the levels of self-esteem, we are amplifying as of today and this is the really fun stuff. There are a large number of ways to now enhance and grow your self-esteem. I am going to start off by looking at some simple and useful ways that have been identified in varying fields of personal development.

I am a bit of a sci-fi fan and I loved all the Star Trek stuff. There was once a sworn foe of the galaxy called 'the Borg' who went around assimilating anyone and anything they could to benefit from them and create a kind of joint consciousness. Please do not worry yourself, we are not going to adopt identical strategies, but today we are going to start to assimilate behaviours.

If you read through your own descriptions about people with self-esteem, or read again the descriptions I have given about how people typically present themselves when they have self-esteem, you actually begin to discover a formula that you can assimilate and use for yourself:

- Stand upright and sit upright.
- Move and manoeuvre in a precise, deliberate, purposeful manner.
- Make eye contact with people (70% of the time is usual for western cultures).

Within my seminars and consulting with companies and individuals, I meet lots and lots of new people and over the years I have begun to get a gut feeling, as we all tend to, about people simply from details such as these obvious ones I have stated.

One of the things that has been discovered and well documented in many fields of modern personal development over recent years is that if you do the things a confident person does, as they would do them, you then actually start to feel more confident yourself. It is very clever stuff.

This is known as *behaving as if*. You can begin to do this in all aspects of your life and at many levels. Use it in your professional or personal life in a variety of ways. Walk up to someone *as if* you expected a certain response. Talk to your bank manager or the person serving you in a shop *as if* you wanted them to treat you with respect and understand your needs. Of course, remember to stand tall, relax your shoulders and move with a sense of purpose, adopt a progressive stance and then you are ready.

I am a big fan of the work of a UK based entertainer, TV mentalist Derren Brown and on his television show one time, he went to a race track and bought tickets for the races and then acted as if he had a winning ticket. He then went and collected winnings from the counter. He was paid out time and time again by the cashiers when his tickets were not winning tickets at all. All because he was so convincing in behaving as if he had won!

This can have an amazing impact on your levels of success as well. When talking, get eye contact with the people you are talking to; speak more deliberately and with more meaning and feel free to express yourself. You do find that as you make these changes consciously to the way you behave and act in the world, you naturally feel more confident. This creates a powerful and favourable cycle of positive behaviour because as you naturally feel more confident, this new behaviour becomes more natural and occurs more naturally too. This is exciting stuff, at least I get excited by it, you see what you are doing here is throwing one heck of a big spanner in the works and interrupting the old patterns of behaviour. In fact, you have turned it around and it is you that has done it!

Now We Build Upwards!

The way in which you behave and the feelings that you have affect each other. Your behaviour often shows what your feelings are and your behaviours also affect how you feel (and vice versa of course). Very often, people think that they have to feel different before they change any of their behaviours. However, it is often far, far easier to do it the other way around.

An individual that has low self-esteem may well focus upon things in their life which have failed or gone wrong rather than focusing on their successes or things they have done well. In a given identical situation or circumstance, someone with a high level of self-esteem will look for what they did well, they will then be proud, and continue to remind themselves of their achievement or their success. They use their own resources, their own progressive and positive thoughts and successful experiences as a way of continually enhancing their energy and motivation.

Project for today: Today's project is fairly substantial and involves you heightening your awareness of your sense of self.

We are going to take stock properly today, think and assess what you have learnt so far. Then I want you to follow these simple steps to start us off on the brain updating process:

- Have a good think about a success that you have experienced or something that went really well or maybe a significant achievement in your life or an every day achievement (is there really such a thing?). As you think about it, think about what it was that has been so successful about it and also notice that thinking about it makes you feel better. Notice what you thought, what internal dialogue you had, where in your body the feelings were, what you saw and heard and how you behaved. With a full, sensory rich idea of your successes you can learn from them and replicate them.
- Run through that entire process again with another occasion. Repeat it a couple of times for both times. Really do this. Invest some energy into your success here.
- Give yourself some praise. Go on, go ahead and praise yourself. Pat yourself on the back! This is nourishing, it is nurturing your

relationship with yourself and rewarding and leads to you building your self-esteem. Have some laughs as you do it, I know I find it hard to keep a straight face when I am doing this.

- Now, start piling on the encouragement. Remember when we did this before? Give yourself some really good encouragement. Encouraging yourself gives you more and more resources for the challenges and difficulties that may lie ahead. As we did earlier, think about how you would encourage someone else and then deliver that encouragement to you.

- Next up is comfort. Now I am not talking about the kind of comfort that I get when I sit in my lovely reclining chair, although it is very nice. I digress. Comfort yourself about something that may have not gone as you wanted. Heal those old wounds that used to be there. Take some time out to nurture yourself and heighten your own personal awareness of self. Accepting and heightening your awareness of these things rather than resisting and fighting past things will allow you to start to take yourself to a new place in the future.

- Remind yourself of your past successes again; remember those things that went well. This can be anything by the way. You are now creating a better internal environment for yourself; you are painting the internal workings of your mind with success and good things. In the past you may have kept on sowing seeds with negative thoughts and reminders, now you choose to do something different.

- Finally, I want you to once again just remind yourself of a happy moment or a time when you felt really good about yourself. There are lots of them. If you are trying your hardest to convince yourself that you cannot recall any good feelings, then email me, I will tell you one of my favourite and irresistible jokes and you'll then have a moment of happiness to cherish. This process helps to change your state. Get used to doing this. Whenever you imagine something really vividly, something that made you feel really good, you cannot help but make changes in your neurology and your physiology. Fabulous stuff.

Please do all these things several times before carrying on. We need to do these simple things to build a basis and a foundation for your success in developing your self-esteem. Please, please hit the pause button with your reading progress. I know there are those of you out there reading this that are not doing these projects properly. Now, even if you firmly believe that doing these things is not going to be successful. If you are being down and miserable about this process, do these things. Just do them. Run through them, push your brain, get uncomfortable; do these things and the following material will serve you infinitely better. Promise yourself that you will do these things before you carry on. Thank you.

Day Eleven

Rain before seven, fine before eleven.

Mid nineteenth century proverb

OK, you did that didn't you? If not, please go back and run through all those things. I cannot express how important it is. If you are not doing as I suggest, then you are unlikely to get all that you want to get from this book. Right then, let us crack on, in fact let's get really advanced.

Accepting You

One of the real foundations of enhanced self-esteem is learning to accept yourself; the notion of self-acceptance. By that I mean accepting yourself as you really are. I am not talking about an unauthentic or false way of doing this which may cause incongruence, nor do I mean pretending to yourself that you are perfect in any way; it is only Mary Poppins and I that are practically perfect in this world.

What I am talking about is the true meaning of that term: accepting yourself as you are. **As you are!** There are lots and lots of pieces of literature documenting evidence from various therapeutic schools that demonstrate that when individuals learn to accept themselves honestly and without blame, without continually criticising themselves and their own perceived failings and weaknesses, they begin to be able to develop and change in a way that pleases them.

With his client centred therapy, the prominent therapist Carl Rogers said 'I find that when I stop trying to change myself, then it happens'. This idea is so often found to be true by many therapists that I speak to about their work, because trying to change yourself suggests some sort of effort on your part is needed. That in turn may well involve overcoming some internal conflict

84

or resistance. When you stop trying, you stop resisting; you are stopping fighting and allowing good things to happen. Yes indeed, you stop resisting. Of course that does not necessarily mean that you do not want to change, but it does mean that you achieve it in a different way, a more wonderfully enjoyable way.

It is often the case that people assume that willpower and teeth gritted determination will take them there. These people make valiant attempts to force themselves to their destination. You are sure to find that willpower is far more effective, exponentially more effective when all of you, you entire self is behind the change you want to make. Ooh, get me, 'exponentially'. If we try to force ourselves, it is really only an attempt by one part of ourselves to overcome another part. We create a kind of civil war within ourselves; each part of ourselves pulling in different directions. I am going to explain this more fully.

Joining Together

If you happen to have two or more parts of yourself that seem to be in conflict with each other, it is important that you realise that all parts of yourself do, in fact, have a good and valid role to play in one way or another. Each and every part of ourselves is trying to achieve something for us, or help us or protect us in some way. It is very useful to suppose from today onwards that all of your behaviours have a positive intention of some sort behind them. That's right; all behaviours have a positive intention of some sort. Who would believe it eh?

We can create such harmony within ourselves by becoming aware of this idea. Absolutely wonderful things can begin to happen when we stop trying to overrule one part of ourselves or another and actually seek to discover what each part of us actually wants for us. This might be seeming a bit confusing, so let me explain some more.

If we have some kind of internal conflict inside our mind between our willpower and the part of us that is resisting; like when someone wants to stop smoking because they know how much more healthy they are going to be, but a part of them enjoys the fact that they get time out at work for a smoking break with friends from another department. Two parts of yourself want conflicting things.

85

In the context here then, when you are trying to achieve a particular result using your willpower you are often really just trying to impose something that you want to happen onto some other part of yourself that has a different outcome or result in mind. For the most part, willpower is what the conscious mind wants or thinks it should do, whereas the objections and resistances to that are coming from other parts of you. Let me illustrate what I mean, again using the example of smoking.

I once worked with a man who came to see me to stop smoking. I used hypnosis and some other personal development techniques to help him stop; I even have a one-to-one programme and I give a personal guarantee for life of its success! Anyway, he wanted to get a good idea about what he was gaining from smoking, what were the by-products for him? We worked together and realised that among other things smoking was a reward for him, it was a distraction when he was under pressure at work, it gave him time to think and a change of scene. It often also gives people a sense of being grown up, or it provides them with something to do with their hands at certain times. With this chap, it also gave him a sense of special friendship with his fellow smoking colleagues that would all take smoking breaks together at work. Subsequently, every time he made a decision to stop smoking, all these combined needs got in the way and barred his way to success. So, we found alternative ways to have those needs met, ways which were healthier than smoking. He then stopped smoking with ease.

Even behavioural responses which seem to be quite negative have a powerful positive intention behind them.

I once worked with a lady who had a fear of balloons. I know, it is very unusual. She was so afraid of balloons that over the years she had decided to hardly ever leave her home in case she saw a balloon. Now, when I worked with her, we discovered that when she was very young, her parents were taking her shopping and a new department store was opening in the town centre and she had been given a balloon with the department store logo on it, you know the kind of thing. They then went to the supermarket for food shopping. While they were shopping, she let go of the balloon by mistake and went to grab it and as she grabbed it, it burst. It popped and shocked her. I mean, I still get shocked if I hear a balloon popping and am not prepared for it. As it popped she turned around and her parents had just gone into the next aisle without realising. She acquainted the fear and shock with her parents disappearing. Some weeks later when she went to a friend's birthday party, her father said to all her friends, 'Oh, don't allow her near the balloons, she is terrified of them.' Good old Dad eh? Then over the years, she had developed more and more of a fear of balloons and buried this experience.

When we explored this experience that she had subsequently buried and forgotten about for all those years, she made herself aware that her fear was actually valid in terms of her experience and that made her feel much, much better about herself. She was able to get more help from me to deal with this outdated response that had been hindering her for years. My point here is that at one stage, the behaviour was valid, it served a purpose back then and when trying to get better, one part of her knew it was ridiculous to fear seeing a balloon, another part of her remembered that it was useful to have a fear of balloons that she had learnt when she was young.

I used all kinds of techniques with her which helped her to overcome her fear in a relatively short period of time. She had realised that even though it was appropriate in the original circumstances, her fear had become so generalised that she was fearful of simply encountering a balloon and that seemed to trigger her fear; just the thought of it! A week later she was out with friends and family enjoying being outdoors once again.

What I want to illustrate here is that these changes have a key notion behind them and that is accepting that the unwanted behaviour or feelings have validity, rather than disliking and attempting to resist them and fight them. Learn to accept yourself as you are, accept that your behaviours have a good intention behind them in some way.

Have a think about someone in your life that you love and know well. I am sure that they are not perfect at all, not like me and Mary Poppins. In fact, I am guessing that if you think about it, they may well have certain quirks or habits that get on your nerves at certain times. However, I am also guessing (there's a lot of guesswork going on here; all scientific of course) that you would not want them to change too much: their irritating behaviours or quirks may in fact just be the other side of a quality or a behaviour that you truly admire, or that is tremendously useful or helpful. So, as of today, allow yourself to begin to develop that same overall tolerance, or acceptance of yourself, with your interwoven good and bad qualities, useful and non-useful qualities. I know you can.

Write down your answers to these questions; if someone else behaved like you do, would you be able to just accept it as just a part of their unique self? Even if you wanted them to change this behaviour in some way, would you still accept them on the whole?

Now, if you found that you answered 'yes' to either or both of these questions, while criticising the same behaviour or quality in yourself, then you are working with a different, far more critical standard for yourself than for everybody else. Now that is not fair on you, is it?

This is quite common. So go ahead and ask yourself, when you think about this quality or behaviour in someone else, just how do you go about finding it acceptable, understandable, and forgivable? Do you, for example, just see it as eccentric? Or do you remind yourself of other things they do which you like? Are you aware that it doesn't happen very often, that it is not bad enough to outweigh all the good things about them? Well? What happens when you treat yourself and your limitations in the same way? So go ahead and find out. Write down answers to all these questions and explore the answers.

Be Nice to Yourself; You Matter

Lots of people are impatient with themselves. It is very likely that if you are continually impatient with yourself, continually have a lack of self-importance or lack worthiness, then you are of course delivering the wrong kind of message to yourself. I mean, just imagine if someone else ignored you or treated you as if you were not important enough. How does that feel? So why oh why do some people insist on ignoring or dismissing themselves?

So, in contrast to that, if you continually deliver the message to yourself you do really matter, you subsequently begin to feel more and more valid and worthwhile. So start caring for yourself and listening to yourself and paying attention to your own needs for starters.

Proving to Yourself That You Do Matter

With the beginning of each new day, begin to take some time out to heighten your awareness of how you are on the inside, what you are feeling and what your thoughts are. Before you set out on your day, take some time out to notice how you are feeling at that moment and compare that to how you are feeling at different times during your day. Let yourself know at the outset of the day just what is important to you for this day ahead and think about what you can do for yourself and what is important to you to do with the day ahead. Of course also let yourself know what it is that will show you that you have achieved something with your day. Have a think about what you will be seeing, hearing and feeling when you achieve what you want to achieve. Create some well-formed outcomes in your mind for the day; you remember well-formed outcomes, don't you?

Then, as each day progresses, keep your daily well-formed outcomes in the forefront of your mind. Make a conscious decision and effort to take progressive steps towards achieving those outcomes for the day. Some people may find that in the initial stages of developing their self-esteem, it is difficult to really nurture themselves. If that happens to be the case with you, then start to be interested about what is preventing you from looking after yourself, exactly how did you manage to avoid, overlook or defer, the things that you wanted or aimed to achieve for yourself? This information is important to you, because it is indicative to you just how you currently harm your self-esteem and may be affecting your own success in enhancing it.

I know that you have victories and successes punctuating every day of your life. When you do experience a success or have an achievement, however insignificant you may initially think it is, take that time out to truly appreciate and recognise what you have done. Even if it is just admiring the shine of your well-cleaned car, finishing a chapter of a book, getting your point of view across to someone or making someone smile, then go and carry on with your day noticing more of the same.

If, on the increasingly rare occasions that something goes in a way that you interpret to be badly, then just continue to use your now increasingly progressive internal dialogue in a style, tone and manner that recognises what you have actually accomplished, achieved or what went really well yesterday, or the day before if not today. Then you can also go about the process of setting it right. Remember, and this is important; your behaviour is not the same thing as your identity. How you behave is not who you are. If you happen to have made a mistake, it certainly does not mean that there is something wrong with you as a person. Be sure to separate out your behaviour from who you are; it means that you can learn from and correct the mistake without feeling it's about who you are. That is not who you are. Have I got that message across enough?

I mentioned that you need to create some outcomes for your day and set your stall out early for each day, to ensure that you measure and keep on track with achieving more each day and of course, keeping track of your beliefs about yourself. It is then equally important in these early days of conditioning your mind for success, that you take some time out at the end of your days too. Not always to do a whole load more analysis, but to show yourself that you are important to you; whether it is going for a jog, meditating, just relaxing and enjoying some quiet, cooking something nice for yourself or walking the dog. If you are one of those people that 'can't find the time' for yourself, then think about how this affects your self-esteem.

Project for today: As we did before, ask yourself some questions, write the answers down and run through the exercises:

- What happened to you today that pleased you?
- How do you know that? What were the details, engage yourself in those moments, remember the things that you saw, what you heard, what words were used, what feelings did you have? Rerun those moments over and over in your mind.
- Reflect on the good things that were said to you or about you during this day. Rerun any compliments you have received, replay them over and over again inside your mind.
- Start to look forward to your day tomorrow. How would you like it to be? Create a film of it inside your mind and imagine some of your outcomes for tomorrow and then run that film over and over; this can be done in a fairly short period of time, it does not have to take an age, make it enjoyable, fun and as brief as you like.

Day Twelve

The wind plays up; snow flutters down.
Twelve men are marching through the town.
Alexander Blok, *The Twelve* (1918)

Taking responsibility for your own thoughts, words, and actions is more easily said than done. However, I believe the quality of your wellbeing is directly proportional to how much self-responsibility you are willing to take. When we blame others or outside events for our position or condition in life we lock ourselves into a prison of pain. There truly is freedom in taking ownership for how we respond to what happens to us in life.

How do successful people react and respond when problems arise? What about those people with high levels of self-esteem? Of course, there are likely to be those occasions when we do make a mistake of some kind, or maybe find ourselves in sticky situations of our own making. Again, we can observe and model successful people and those with high self-esteem to indicate to ourselves that there are a wide variety of ways that these people use to overcome any issues or problems as they occur. Anyone can learn how to replicate these insights and strategies.

As I mentioned earlier, one of the key things to learn here is to separate the things that you do from your own identity. What you do is not who you are. Of course, it is extremely valuable for you to be aware that although you are responsible for your own actions, your behaviour is just an attempt to achieve certain goals that you have. It may not always be the best way to achieve those goals and it may sometimes need to be altered. Do just continue to have in the forefront of your mind the belief that you are much more than what you do or how you behave.

Again, look to identify what the positive intention is behind any behaviour; that can be the behaviour of yourself or other people. The vast majority of your behaviour is purposeful; some would

91

even suggest that all behaviour is purposeful. Really do your best to recognise and be as aware as possible of the positive intention in all behaviours. When you do recognise the positive intention, it achieves two main things for you:

- It ensures that you have information about something you really need or want or what is really important to you; maybe you were not aware of it in this situation.
- Once you are aware of what it is you really want, you can usually find more constructive ways of going about it.

For example, a fear of something often has the positive intention of protecting yourself from that thing. You can test this out on other people too; work out what others may be trying to achieve by their unusual or obnoxious behaviours. This can give you that kind of information. Often, you can get a change in others when you are able to give them alternative means for achieving the same end. Get it really clear in your mind; what is within your power to change? Think about what your choices are to get that in a different way.

How Do You Think?

We are going to be looking at the workings of your mind in far greater detail on a later day in this book, however, today you are going to begin to examine your thoughts and look at the ways in which you may or may not leave certain pieces of information out of your thoughts. By that, I am referring to the things that we forget, times when we ignore warning signs or maybe when we are not fully paying attention. Then, on the positive side we sometimes do not notice unpleasant surroundings when we are with the ones we love; these kinds of thought processes are called deletions. Today, notice if you delete things in your mind.

Also, as you continue to examine your thoughts, you also want to consider if you make universal or really broad claims based on a limited amount of information. By that I mean that some people may think that the entire world is against them; are you sure everyone is against you? Even people that have never met you? I can remember when following my first ever paid motivational speaking engagement at a company's annual conference, I had been received really well, got a standing ovation and instantly told everyone that I was a brilliant presenter as a result of this one experience! These things are called generalisations and something that we all do.

Finally, as you examine your own thoughts notice also how it is that you create meaning by focusing on some kinds of information and ignoring others; you remember Arthur and Annie from our earlier examples? Another example of this type of thing is that a man may see an ex-lover joking and laughing with a friend and assumes they are laughing about him, or where your partner buys you a special surprise gift and you decide that you just know they are in love with you. We call these things distortions. When examining and considering deletions, generalisations and distortions in your thoughts, do the following to make this easier:

- Firstly, accept yourself as you are.
- Secondly, really pay attention to your day-to-day experience. Stop dismissing or overlooking things that are a part of your day-to-day experience. Even the smallest of difficulties can alert you to things that need updating or changing.
- Remember to get the idea into your head, that everything, even the most unusual or self-destructive behaviour has a purpose or a positive intention: check out and examine what the behaviour might be trying to do for you.

Being Instinctive and Intuitive

Did you ever get a 'gut feeling' about something? Of course you did. Learning to listen to that feeling and that sense is a really important way of developing your sense of self and it is a vast source of unconsciously processed information. It is our unconscious mind communicating with us and it is so important to listen to it and to trust it. Your unconscious mind works so very much faster than the conscious mind and our bodies reflect this and we get feelings as it communicates with us.

It is like when we get one of those sinking sensations that indicates to us that we are uncertain, or displeased about a particular situation or event. Be sure that you are heightening your awareness of this, when people ignore this it can be very much to their detriment. Instead, choose to really tune into it, even make a note of it and what you think it is telling you. Do this prior to reacting or making choices or decisions about what you are unconsciously communicating to yourself via your intuition and instincts. There is always sure to be some insightful and highly useful information in that sensation about how you truly feel and what you truly want. When you have such a wonderful, naturally occurring resource, I think it is madness to ignore it and not utilise it as much as possible.

These things that start out as 'gut feelings' take time to be understood or appreciated for what they are. They also take their time to develop into something that your conscious mind can easily understand and use: so be patient and give yourself as much time as you possibly can to translate them.

What Do You Want?

We have learnt about this notion already, but I want to give you a couple of important reminders here. Now, your goals may well seem ever changing. I know that many of my own goals seem to change daily. You may well alter and change your goals when there are good reasons to do so. Before doing that though, it is vitally important to know what you want. Maybe, even more importantly, answer the question 'what do you want?' By reminding you of this at this stage, I want to encourage you to build a very valuable habit of self-consultation. Regularly heightening your awareness of your existence and noting the importance of your own consultation in turn enhances your self-esteem and ability to attract the kind of life you want.

Think about and imagine how someone else would feel if you consistently neglected to ask them how they were or what they wanted. You can also imagine what kind of a problem that would cause in any relationship if you never asked the other person how they felt or what they wanted. I think everyone can find it easy to see and imagine how they could come to feel unwanted, unimportant or even worthless. Of course, the very same applies to the way that you treat yourself. Treating yourself as though you matter is the quickest way to help you feel that you do matter. Remember earlier when we mentioned about letting yourself know that you matter?

So, the reason for these reminders here is that these things in turn lead you to behave as though you matter in your interaction with others in the world outside. Keep this in the forefront of your mind. When people act as if they matter, other people tend to respond accordingly (like the Miss Piggy theory mentioned earlier). So by first treating yourself as though you really do matter, you are creating a wonderfully powerful ripple of positivity which spreads further and further and wider into your world and your life.

Keeping Track of Where You Are At

I have been self-employed for so many years now that I think I am verging on being unemployable for regular employment. I have not actually had many jobs, but I can remember at one of my very first jobs, my line manager telling me 'You have a lot to learn', he was naturally fed up at the time with the fact that I used to constantly make jokes at his expense in front of an office full of people who were fearful of behaving like I did and were amazed that I got away with it. Now, the reason I mention this is because if someone tells you 'you have a lot to learn' which happens a lot in life, you want to make sure that you interpret the progressive ramifications of what is being said to you and recognise positive implications as well as any intended negative ones. Let me give you an example of what I mean; you can think to yourself that 'you have a lot to learn' and add something progressive and positive to that statement such as *'before you are in a position to ...* take up a role with more responsibility, get married and have children, or in my case back then; think I could run the entire company at the age of 21.

This notion does not have to stop there. You need to make a conscious decision to stop translating the statement into 'what he means is that I don't know much at all', even if you are pretty sure that is what the intention of the statement was. What I want to impress here is that what we believe is a construction in our own head; we concentrate on beliefs towards the end of the book by the way. We create our beliefs and they are based upon our understanding of our own world. If our experience and the way we interpret the world around us is actually something we construct, it makes sense to instead construct a reality that is far, far more positive and progressive and useful rather than us limiting ourselves. Now, am I right or am I right here?

This does not mean that we have to become unrealistic or verge on silliness. If your manager, or parent or coach thinks that you have a lot to learn, be aware of it in a way that is for your better good and be realistic. Just insist on reminding yourself that things can be learnt. A great way forwards is to consider asking that person exactly what they think you need to learn in order to move forward in the way they think; ensure that it is appropriate to do so of course.

You know what I always used to think to myself? To say that I had a lot to learn showed that he thought I was capable of doing so, he must have thought I was capable of learning and developing! So take that progressive decision today to ensure that you give yourself something really useful to learn from every exchange and you are then maintaining and developing your self-esteem at the same time as opening you to more success in developing your self-esteem.

The Stance of Your Sense of Self

How do you view the world? I want to run an idea past you about how you perceive the world around you. Your perception of any experience depends on the position from which you perceive it. I am going to mention three positions here that are useful to your use with building self-esteem and success. They are known quite simply as the first, second and third positions:

- In the first position you are in your own body, looking out through your own eyes, seeing things from your own point of view.
- Being in the second position means stepping into someone else's shoes, imagining what it is like to be them, looking at the world through their eyes.
- The third position is taking the stance of a third person that is viewing events in which you are involved, a bit like being a fly on the wall (how many times have I wanted to do that?).

You see, taking a different perceptual position enables you to step out of what you are currently experiencing. It allows you to see things from a different perspective and gather different kinds of information. You can also keep a keen eye on how your own behaviour might be affecting other people, and then of course how they might feel about you. Taking different positions enables you to access information that your unconscious mind already has that you may have been overlooking. You can be aware of things that you may not have been consciously aware of before.

So, on an average day in addition to keeping aware of your ongoing experience of life as I have been suggesting by taking time to notice what you feel, what you want, seeing from inside your own eyes in the first position. Then, wonder what it is like to be someone else in the same situation, from the second position. Imagine how other people might see this experience; this is especially useful if that person was someone you know who has a good level of self-esteem and attracts success. Thirdly then, see yourself and others as if from an outside perspective, looking at the larger picture as in the third position. Then you can think of using this idea of taking different perceptual positions when you encounter any kind of conflict or when planning a project or evaluating a situation or if you ever feel stuck on something.

I can remember when I trained for my first marathon, I thought that I would not be able to complete it in the time that I had wanted to do. During a conversation with my Mum, she told me that I was the kind of person that always did things in a very focused way when I set my mind on it. It was not for a few years that I realised something about what she said to me.

Often when we feel a certain way about something, it is quite common for our friends and family to be able to see our strengths and values when we ourselves don't. We can use this to benefit us and to access our confidence if we are ever lacking it or doubt ourselves as I was.

Project for today: Here is an exercise to do. Your project today is simply to follow it and complete it.

Firstly, close your eyes and think of someone who really and sincerely loves you or someone who really appreciates you in some way. Remember how they look and imagine them standing or sitting in front of you.

Then, imagine stepping out of your body and into the body of the person who loves you. Look through their eyes, hear through their ears and feel their love and good feelings as they look at you.

Thirdly, notice in some fine detail what it is that they love and appreciate about you. Fully understand these wonderful and beautiful qualities that perhaps you had overlooked or had not appreciated in the same way before. Take some time to really feel good as you look at yourself through those eyes.

Next up, notice whereabouts in your body that the feeling is the strongest and then give that feeling a colour; it can be the colour that you think most suits the feeling, let it happen without too much thought.

Now, imagine spreading that colour all the way through your body and mind, spreading into every cell, from top to toe, toe to top, left to right and back again, fill your entire being with it.

Now double its intensity and brightness. Really concentrate on doing this now. Then, open your eyes and do keep that lovely, glowing feeling inside of you.

I have often kept that feeling inside for hours on end. Do this exercise over and over and continue to boost those feelings more and more. The more that you do it, the easier and better it becomes and will soon become an automatic belief about yourself. You'll feel more loved and more appreciated and this will boost your confidence and self-esteem.

Day Thirteen

It was a bright cold day in April, and the clocks
were striking thirteen.

George Orwell, *Nineteen Eighty Four* (1949)

I am sure that you have encountered plenty of people who both
professionally and personally tend to put the needs of others
before themselves. For many it is an integral aspect of their work
whereas some learn this way of being during their younger years.
The variety of carers in our society learn how to minimise taking
notice of their own feelings in order to take care of their clients
and patients. People that tend to drive themselves into fatigue,
depression or even illness include individuals such as hospital
doctors working ridiculously long hours, high ranking city execu-
tives responding to their bosses, mothers to their young children,
teachers within schools and colleges and managers of large
companies with lots of employees. With these kinds of people,
because of their beliefs about what their role entails, they have a
habit of putting the needs of the company or the client first. There
can then come a point where these kind of people do not even
notice their own feelings.

This is potentially dangerous. This kind of attitude to oneself
produces conscious and unconscious attempts to take care of the
self in short term ways or ways that are detrimental to our own
well-being, including smoking or drinking alcohol or eating too
much or the wrong things. These things then replace the good,
direct and long-term ones. People often try to give themselves
quick treats, but in a way that can erode their self-esteem or your
ability to attract success as you find that you cannot go without it,
and also these things do not create natural good feelings most of
the time.

So then what happens is that the teacher leaves the profession,
the executive gets burnt out early, the nurse goes sick with

constant illness, and the doctor chooses to work in a private clinic with regular hours and pleasant surroundings. All of these may well be valid, but if they are not the individual's choice and they are forced decisions, it really does nothing for your sense of self.

Putting oneself first actually means that we are then in a far better position to look after others. If we are fit and well and happy, we have plenty spare for others. We can give generously, without minding. Putting time and energy into building your self-esteem and levels of success is one of the most wonderful investments that you can make. So, we want to start getting you to notice you.

What Do You Like About You?

Is there someone in your life that you truly admire or think a lot of? What is it about them that you like so much? Stop and have a think about them for a moment. Really think about the reasons you like them so much. I am sure that some of you may have responded with that old chestnut 'I just do'. Now whether you are consciously aware of it or not, there are more reasons than that. I am positive that you could come up with lists and lists of amazing qualities that you find likeable in others. Liking someone involves identifying and enjoying certain qualities that you appreciate and think highly of. This is why we end up liking people that we are unlikely to actually meet but are in the public eye. You can respect someone without liking them; liking them is to enjoy them.

Rather than sounding like some guide for making friends, I thought I would explain what is meant by all this; this is very similar to the process of liking oneself. As I have already mentioned, liking comes from having a true sense of self-acceptance; we do not have to be perfect model citizens. Your liking for yourself will increase once you know more about how you function and learning to accept yourself as you are, even if you do have issues or foibles every now and then.

Now have a think about popular public figures. Very often one of the things that continues to draw people to them is not their accomplishments but the fact that they have frailties and foibles.

This is what so many of the popular glossy magazines focus on, showing the regular lives and problems of the famous and it is one of the reasons that people seem to be so drawn to reality television programmes such as 'Big Brother'. It is as if the message is 'look, they are just like us'. We see how human other people really are.

Therefore, it is this process of being drawn to what makes people human and real and that shows them to be fallible at times that works between us and other people; surely it can also work inside of ourselves. Actually, it can be a relief to allow ourselves to accept any limitations that we may think we have and even become fond of them, even proud, as long as they are not interfering too much with our lives.

Enjoying Yourself

That's right, as of this very day, you are moving on to starting to enjoy being yourself. What are the things that you do enjoy about the way you are? At the end of the day, when taking stock of your day, you can also take some time to ask yourself what you most liked about you today. Do include everything, even if it was a small, supposedly non-important thing. Perhaps you wore a certain handkerchief because it matched a new shirt? You must have been bought one that is in a drawer somewhere that your great auntie bought you several Christmas's ago! Perhaps it was something that you did, an enjoyable or beneficial interaction you had, or perhaps it was even something that you chose not to do or something that you thought.

My immediate family are always joking about how my grand-dad chuckles away to himself in the corner of the room as he remembers things that make him laugh. My Nana tells him off for doing so, but it is hilarious to see him being like that.

In a similar vein to some things you have done previously, I now want you to make an official list in your journal that begins 'I like myself because .. '. Then make another list that begins 'I like ... about myself'. Of course, you then have to add to those lists.

So think of the people you like the most, as we did before, and the people who like you the most. If they like you, dare to trust that you are actually well worth liking, and then dare to like yourself as they do. Go on, I dare you!

Similarly, but much more comprehensively than we did before I now want you to write a list that begins 'I like myself because . . .'. Then make another list that begins 'I like . . . about myself'.

Are You In a State?

Today, I want to start getting you into a state. You are always in some kind of a state, though we are often not consciously aware of it. A state is your way of being at any given moment. It involves what is happening in your brain, what is going on in your body, what you are seeing, doing, feeling and what you are thinking.

Before we go further with this, I want you to think about one of the times in the past when you had what I refer to as 'one of those days'. Let me give you an example. As I mentioned before, I worked for a national newspaper in central London when I was much younger and I commuted from outside of London. One day, I slept through my alarm clock and woke late. I was running late and caught the train during the busiest time of day when there were more people than I was used to with my earlier train. I could not get a seat, so had to stand for the entire journey and could not read my newspaper to update myself with them, as was an essential part of my job, my routine was disrupted. Upon arrival in the city, I grabbed a coffee and raced for the underground which was packed, I mean it was heaving.

I was nose to nose with people that I did not want to be. I eventually got into work about an hour late. My boss rushed over, would not accept any excuses, told me off and told me he expected the report that I had to give him today by 11am. I rummaged through my bag to realise that I had left it on my table at home where I had been up all night working on it. So, I have another coffee and ignore all of the messages from my worst clients that are fuming that I am not returning their calls. I went and told my boss about the report and he gave me a full written warning that went on my files and I had to go home and get it.

When I got back, people were ranting, my boss was not impressed with my report, etc, etc. More coffee, nothing to eat, more stress. My best friend at work, the girl on the next desk, leaned over, smiled assuringly and understandingly and asked if she could borrow a paper clip as she had run out, to which I replied, 'Look, can you just get lost! For Christ's sake!'

I had things out of perspective. I went into a rage when my best friend had asked me for a paper clip. It was ridiculous, she still reminds me about that day now. What I wanted to introduce with that story of me foaming at the mouth and going temporarily insane with stress, is that I was in a state.

Usually when we say that we are in a state, we often are referring to something that we think of as intense or negative. Any state that you experience is a merging of a number of psychological and physiological events and behaviours, which last long enough to be recognised as a state of some kind. A state may involve both particular thoughts and feelings and physiological characteristics such as respiration rate, muscular tension, blood pressure, facial colour and temperature changes.

Now then, I can confirm that some states are pleasant, uplifting and enjoyable, oh yes. Some are divine, ecstatic and blissful. Others may be mild or unpleasant. We like some states and are apprehensive or fearful about others. Good management of our states make us more and more effective in our lives, in addition; it greatly enhances our self-esteem and thus our openness to success.

We tend to develop our own repertoire of states that we are accustomed to such as relaxing when the sun shines, my boss's tone makes me nervous, seeing other people exercising makes me guilty and so on. Sometimes we recognise these states at the time, particularly in relation to specific stimuli. Exams and tests are widely seen as triggering anxiety, our birthdays often make us excited, Christmas or other celebrations often make many people feel good. Some people become euphoric with some things, others can become anxious or filled with dread as they anticipate that event.

One way of accurately monitoring states is to look at them developing in families. So very often, children can be remarkably sensitive gauges of state changes in adults. They really notice and respond accordingly.

I once worked with a lovely married couple who had attended one of my courses and subsequently brought in their daughter to see me. She was having lots and lots of disruptive tantrums and was attention seeking at seemingly innocuous things. The remainder of the time, she was happy, playful and loving. The parents just could not comprehend the behaviour.

So I asked them to begin to pay some detailed attention to when and where these tantrums were happening. They recorded it every time and heightened their awareness of when it occurred and noticed some interesting results. Their daughter's tantrums occurred at times of change in the circumstances; when leaving school, or returning from a friend's house or when it was time for bed or if she had to come in from playing outside.

A variety of things were occurring during these times. The parents made a list of all the possibilities. Of course, there was a change in their own focus at those times and subsequently, the adult's attention shifted from their daughter on to the next thing they had to do. They often felt pressurised; as if there was a greater sense of urgency, they kept thinking they must do this and should be doing that. Then it was as if their daughter was a sponge to all that tension. Both child and parents were creating a circular behaviour of winding each other up because of what they saw in each other and what they anticipated in the other.

Being aware of this occurring pattern was the first step. In order to change it, I asked them to develop and create a similar profile of all the times that they had fun and enjoyed themselves together. They noted down when and how they all were at their best together. They discovered that the times they had the most cohesion and enjoyment was when there were no time constraints, where their activities could be negotiated and where their daughter felt involved and had a say in what they did. She picked up on their more relaxed state and responded accordingly.

So they created a strategy that whenever they collected their daughter from somewhere or had to go somewhere else or something was coming to an end, they would explain the situation to her, that they would be leaving shortly, they kept their concentration and focus on her as much as possible and relaxed in those situations more. She reacted wonderfully and the change was dramatic. They had realised that the tantrums became a kind of measurement for their own changes in state; fascinating stuff.

When considering this example, we can be aware of a great many things creating the overall experience:

- The feelings and states such as pressure, anxiety, relaxation, frustration.
- The pace of the experience; whether things were hurried, forced, or leisurely. This includes thoughts too, thinking that they should do something.
- The non-verbal communication and body language of tension, their speed of movement, tone of voice, degree of focus.

Think about how many times you have been able to identify a person's state without them saying a word. Or if you have ever seen a television programme in a foreign language and still known what was going on from everything else that they communicated about their state.

There are a wide variety of ways that we can alter states that are unpleasant or non-useful and also ways to re-create those wonderful states and useful, productive states. I have concentrated on the negative states so far, to highlight how you can be aware of them and subsequently change them. There are a vast array of fabulous enjoyable states too. The key to maintaining progressive states within yourself is as much about finding out more about your good states, how you created them, how you can have more of them, than trying to avoid unwanted states.

Altering That Perceptual Position Again

OK, so you remember earlier when I was discussing the perceptual positions that we take in life. I want to reinforce the notion of taking the third position. Just as those parents became observant of their behaviours, so recognising your states and managing those states can help you observe and understand your behaviour.

When you change your perceptual position and step into the third position, you step outside of your own map of the world; you dissociate from your own feelings, experiences, beliefs and assumptions and notice what they are. Notice how interesting it can be to observe how you behave. Ask what their behaviour might mean to them as you observe yourself from that position. Notice that they always do certain things at certain times and occasions when certain things happen, notice the patterns within yourself by observing yourself from the third position.

Taking the third position does more than give you a wide range of information. It literally changes your relationship with the situation. When your state is unpleasant or non-useful, taking the third position helps to distance you from it and allows you to dissociate from it. However, when it is a useful, enjoyable state, noticing the detail does something to the contrary; it enhances your awareness of it and immerses you even more in it. You then enjoy it more and you appreciate it more.

Quite often, when someone is not feeling as good as they would like to, they try to distract themselves which often in turn makes them feel worse. When you learn to understand and be aware of your own states, you learn to recognise them, what causes them and you can find yourself in a position of being able to prevent certain states from occurring before they get to an unmanageable level. Heightening awareness of your states helps you to allow you to prevent much of what you don't need and allows you to make more of each moment.

Making a Note of Your States

Now, I don't know about you, but I am quite sure, no, I am really sure that I would not want to spend my life experiencing limiting and unpleasant states, but you would be amazed how many people actually do. Think about how much time you spend in states that you would rather not. What states would you rather be in? As you think about those states that you would like to be in, then think about how much time you actually spend in those states. Note this all down.

I have worked with large numbers of people that do not like to leave their comfort zone. I bet there are some of you reading who would rather not fully immerse yourself in this book and have not been doing the exercises and not been stretching yourself or doing anything different, you may expect results from simply reading the book. Think about how much of your time you spend in your comfort zone. There are states which are unpleasant but necessary because they may be warning you of danger, again, how much time do you spend in those states? Make a graph of some sort and map out how much time you spend in what kind of states. It is really important to see how you lead your life in what states. Where are you spending most of your time? In what state?

Project for today: Write about your existing states. Then look back through your entire lifetime and map out a general idea of the dominant states in periods of your life, then ask yourself some really key questions:

- Does that state remind me of something?
- What age do I feel like when I am in this state?
- What do I really want when I am in this state?
- What is it about this state that tells me I am in it (i.e. Where are those feelings in your body?)
- How do others react to that state?
- What states do you find to be the most enjoyable?
- What states contribute to the most problems in your life?
- What states do you want more of?
- What states do you want to change?

Please, please answer all these questions as thoroughly as you possibly can. This is crucial to your future success. I mean really crucial. Note it all down, take some time to do this and please do not progress until you have completed it to your own satisfaction.

Day Fourteen

*What do we ever get nowadays from reading to
equal the excitement and the revelation in those
first fourteen years?*

Graham Greene,
The Lost Childhood and Other Essays (1951)

State Creation and Development

I want to demonstrate and illustrate how to change and develop
your own states with more and more natural ease. Just because we
have come to think of our states as complex experiences, it does
not mean that the process of changing them is equally complex, in
fact it is quite the opposite. In order to change your own state, you
simply need to recognise the state, change the state and ask
yourself what you really want and I am going to go into each of
these things in more detail.

By recognising what is going on with yourself and tuning into
yourself as you have been doing regularly throughout the various
stages of this book, you give yourself the chance of changing it.
So, if you have not done so already, gather information on your
states, especially your desired states; think about what sets it off,
when it happens, what changes it and who you are with this state
– do you like it, fear it, want to be free of it or are you scared of
losing it?

Changing States

Having recognised a state and being interested in it is often more
than enough to break a state and interrupt it. You may need to
do more than that though. So, here are a set of ideas to help you
to change your state whenever you want to.

Firstly, continue to spend time in the third person. As I
discussed earlier, experience yourself and observe yourself from a
different vantage point as the neutral observer or the 'fly on the

wall'. Get into that different perspective and observe your state and yourself.

Secondly, continue to move your body and alter your physiology. You can change this easily. Move your body differently, change your posture, move around, adopt the positions that you adopt when you feel a different way. I know that when you are happy you hold your body differently to when you are sad, so change your physiology. Really get into the idea of asking yourself what you need to do physiologically to make yourself feel and be different at that time. Interrupt the pattern of that state by breaking it physically.

Thirdly, partake in some time travel. In true Dr Who style, travel through time to experience things from a very different perspective of time. Move yourself away from the here and now and the reality of what you might be experiencing. Instead run a pleasant memory from the past or imagine something happening in the future that you really want to happen. Remember things that are going to happen next week or later on today when you will be in a different state altogether. Imagine a time when a particular problem will be solved. Remember our goal setting and well-formed outcomes? Absorb and immerse yourself in the future you.

Fourthly, notice your state and realise what your state really is. Whatever your experience is, put it into a larger context, see it in the larger scheme of things. If you have just had an argument, remind yourself of all the things that you liked about that person before, and then imagine a time in the future when you are great friends again. If you realise the importance of certain qualities to you in the past, you know that they are important in the future too. Then thank yourself for noticing and learning from the experience and notice how it changes how you feel about it.

Next up, create and develop progressive states. I have often needed to find some inner strength or mental calmness before I can even think about dealing with something that I have to do, especially if it is demanding. Let me tell you how I do that. Sometimes I do something different for a while to build up to it, or I encourage myself to do something and gee myself on, but most of the time I think about how I did something well before and remember the feelings I had then, when I handled something really well and successfully. Sometimes, I create a plan of how to do something if I have not done it before or I think about the state I want and think about how I got it before and then think of that occasion and focus on the feeling. These things all have the possibility of creating more progressive states.

Finally, what is it that sets your states off? Have a good think and work out what it is that sets off your good feelings. How do they start? What makes you feel good? These things that you note are triggers that you imagine thinking of and firing off whenever you want to feel good and set off a good state. I know that sometimes I just have to see a particular person to feel good, or listen to a piece of music or imagine someone's voice in my ear, or I imagine how I feel after I have been involved in a running event. Make another list of all the things that set off your good positive states, then you can use them to activate those states whenever you want to.

Be sure to run through these steps as often as you can.

Transforming Your States

So how do we go about changing and transforming our states? Here is a set of procedures to be able to get yourself into positive, progressive states that then in turn allow you to bolster, boost and enhance your self-esteem.

First of all, tune into and be aware of your states. As discussed in detail already, find out more and more about your states. The reason I keep emphasising this so much is because it is so important. Get aware of the details of your state and ask yourself how you get in to that state. What happened to get you into that state? Think about states of uncertainty, lack of confidence, low self-esteem and diminished value of yourself because there is no place for those states anymore. Focus on how to feel more confident, with a growing sense of self, at peace with yourself, content being you and accepting of who you are, and then work out how you get into those powerful states.

Secondly, tune in to your physiological experiences and be aware of your body. Again, as we discussed, become aware of the physical elements of what you are experiencing. Notice what occurs physically during certain states and experiences. If you keep getting migraines under certain circumstances, learn to know what those circumstances are. Then also ask yourself, what has to happen for those migraines to not happen? What times do they not happen? Think about all your own personal situations relating to your self-esteem and apply this notion to it.

Thirdly then, notice the states of others. Again, to reiterate, be aware of the states of others and ask them questions about their states. Then model what it is that they do well and add this to your own list of achievable and attainable states so that you have more choices for your own states. What you are doing here is studying the kind of states that you want to be in. This really is the height of self-esteem; letting yourself choose how you are moment by moment.

Finally, demand more, more and much more. Take your time to enjoy your good feelings. I mean really experience the good states. Learn how to recreate them and add to them and enrich them and make them better and better. Always look at how to enjoy them more but really appreciate them for what they are now. Work out how to have more good feelings. Then even more and keep working this out. I get excited just thinking about that. The real essence of beautiful state management is allowing yourself to have more good feelings and enjoying them more and how to adjust or alter those that you are not entirely happy with. This is how to have self-esteem, by just feeling wonderful more of the time!

Recreate Feelings, Anchor Them

Have you ever wished you could keep a positive feeling for longer? Ever felt that you wish you could recreate feelings as and when you want to? Well now you can. Just follow these simple steps.

There was some sunshine this weekend while I was writing this! At least here on the sunny south coast of England there was. I went out running along the sea front on Saturday morning and it was wonderful; the feeling of the sunshine on my face, the smell of the air, the sights of other people out and about and happy, the local land train was shuttling people and their excited children back and forth from Bournemouth pier to Boscombe Pier and my senses were filled – a major event for human neurophysiology (mine anyway).

The funny thing is, later on that evening when my friends were joking about my pink coloured forehead, I told them that I was really looking forward to summer and as I spoke, I felt the sun on me, imagined the fun I was going to have on the beach, remembered the smell, the amazing feeling of joy that I get from being there, just by anticipating it all.

An anchor is something that we do, think or experience that creates a stored response within us. In the example I gave regarding myself, I experienced a natural phenomenon we can replicate with these anchoring techniques that I am about to explain. You see, without realising it, the time I had spent on the sea front earlier that day had acted as an anchor for the wonderful experience which immediately followed it. The next time I saw and heard the experience, albeit in my mind, my neurology thought 'I know what happens now' and started to produce the intense physical responses that it expected and believed were coming next.

In the fields of modern personal development, an anchor is any representation in the human nervous system that triggers any other representation. For instance, the word 'sex' will immediately trigger images, sounds and thoughts associated with that word. The word 'chocolate' will trigger different associations. I am not too sure which of those will create the most intense feelings though! These words are anchors. Anchors do not have to be words; they can be a wide range of things.

With this brilliant process, we identify that anchors can operate in any representational system; we can see them, hear them, feel them, smell them and taste these things that activate an automatic response. Let me give you some examples:

- Tonal anchors: By that, I mean for example, the special way a certain person has of saying your name, like when a friend or family member says it. My mother shouting my name from the depths of my home when I was a child often signalled the fact that she had discovered something that I had done that meant trouble for me! 'Adam!' often made me feel what I was in store for.
- Anchors that are tactile: The affect of a certain type of handshake for example, or the sensation of a reassuring hug compared to a loving cuddle. These things rekindle all kinds of wonderful feelings.

- Visual anchors: So for example the way people respond to certain items of clothing that you see someone wearing. I recently had lunch with a group of my friends from the town where I grew up and several of them commented on the jacket I was wearing. Now, whenever they see it, it reminds them of those comments and makes them smile. Mainly because they all joke about it at my expense!
- Olfactory anchors: Like when you smell a certain kind of food being cooked can suddenly have you remembering a time when you were in the school cafeteria.
- Gustatory anchors: The taste of your favourite food or the way certain foods can make you remember how you felt when you had it before. Maybe like when you were given soup and a big helping of love and sympathy when you were young and off school because you were poorly. I know every time I eat Heinz Tomato soup it reminds me of just that.

Once again, in the fields of modern personal development, an anchor is any representation in the human nervous system that triggers any other representation. It is conceptually similar to Pavlov's response conditioning with dogs. He used to ring bells every time the dogs were fed and got to the stage where he would ring the bell without presenting food and he still had a gang of salivating dogs. Now, we do not want to dribble whenever we hear bells, but imagine if we could feel filled with a sense of self-esteem whenever we saw, heard or smelt certain things.

While the anchor I created for the sea front was unintentional, it is possible for you to use this anchoring technique to anchor yourself and your states intentionally. Have a go at this and learn this very clever technique for yourself.

Firstly, think of an occasion when you had a highly pleasurable, positive or enjoyable experience. See what you saw then (looking out through your own eyes), hear what you heard and feel what you felt. As you feel the sensations increase in intensity, squeeze the thumb and forefinger of your dominant hand gently together for a few moments, and then release them.

Now 'break your state' and think of something else away from this exercise, maybe by remembering what you had for lunch yesterday or what shoe you put on first when you put them on today. Now, simply squeeze your thumb and forefinger together again, gently pulsing them. The progressive state will return. This needs practice to make it really effective, but just think about how useful this is going to be when you use this to feel good about yourself more and more often.

To make the most of this anchoring technique, it is important to really engage in the experience and make it wonderfully vivid in your mind and to then also put effort and energy into recalling it when you first activate your anchor for the first few times. You really need to get your brain associating as much as it can with your intended anchor. Imagine how powerful this can be when you want to feel wonderful if you are at home, feeling gloomy. Instead of reaching for the chocolate for example, you can start to activate your 'feel good' anchor.

Every time you want to get motivated to exercise, just activate your enthusiasm anchor. It is a really simple technique of learning to use your own innate resources and your ability to activate the states you want, when you want them.

This is a simple but powerful technique that can enable you to have access to the states and resources you want, when you want them, so you can control how you feel in certain circumstances and begin to create and develop anchors for confidence, self-esteem and all the other progressive states that you know you want more of. The use of thumb and forefinger being squeezed together is an example of a physical tactile anchor, but you can use any representation to anchor something for yourself or someone else.

Guidelines for Setting Anchors for Yourself

In order to get a 'strong' anchor for an experience, it is important to:

- Ensure that you have a powerful example of the experience to work with.
- Anchor in as many representational systems as possible, so use sights, sounds images, smells, tastes and feelings when you are setting an anchor.
- Set the anchor just before the experience peaks. Just a moment before it is due to be at it's height in your mind, set the anchor

(i.e. by squeezing your thumb and forefinger together) at that moment.

One of the people who came on one of my recent training courses was particularly taken with the idea of anchoring. Shortly after the seminar, one morning his wife offered to make him a cup of tea, and as she did so, he gently tapped the side of his cup with his ring. He repeated this the next few times she made him a cup of tea. After a while, all he had to do was tap the side of his cup subtly with his ring and she would spontaneously offer to get him a cup of tea!! Very naughty use of the technique, eh?! Just by creating a sensory representation (tapping the cup) that coincided with her making tea, he was soon able to use that representation as a trigger for what he wanted. He did eventually share his anchoring experience with his wife and you can be sure he makes a lot more tea than she does now!

Now I know that by now some of you may be thinking 'But isn't that manipulative?' One answer is 'yes, so use it for doing good stuff.' Use it to make yourself and others feel good and develop your sense of self-esteem. Another answer is 'no'. It is no more manipulative than making yourself look good and smell nice when you go out. In those situations you are trying to get people to think the best of you and have a good response to you, a response that you are attempting to anchor through your choice of clothing, grooming and smelly perfume.

Here are some of the sorts of things that I go out of my way to use to anchor whenever I see them or experience them:

- Smiles.
- Laughter.
- Excitement.
- Confidence.
- Good feelings.
- Good performance (especially by waiters and waitresses!).
- Anything that looks good, useful or fun; achievement and success are especially useful for stopping smoking, reducing weight or growing in confidence.

If you keep anchoring the good experiences that occur in your life, you will be more and more able to actually recreate them at will and have far more resources available for feeling good about yourself more and more of the time. What's more, it is happening all the time anyway.

As I said at the beginning, anchoring is a naturally occurring phenomenon anyway. You are exposed to it all the time in everything you do. Everyone is doing this stuff all the time, often without really knowing it. All I am inviting you to do is to become conscious of the anchors that you and others are setting, and to start using them purposefully to get good results, rather than randomly to get whatever you get. Use this technique with mindfulness.

Taking This a Step Further

Recently, I was working with a team of staff members with regards to doing some consulting with them. I asked them how they would know that the two days had been a great success. One of them said it would have a 'feel good factor' and simultaneously made a gesture with both hands towards his tummy. When I repeated the words 'feel good factor?' to him, he nodded in confirmation. Later on, I referred to the feel good factor, and simultaneously used his gesture. Instead of a nod of confirmation, I got a full physiological response, including skin colour changes, posture and energy changes; he really responded with the full works. Hearing his own words being fed back to him had been a good anchor, but the words plus the gesture were far more complete. When I used both, I got a full physical response from him in return. I continued to use the anchor throughout the consultation. At no time was he aware that I was using his anchors – he just had the experience of being really well understood.

This book is not about how to go about doing this with other people; I want you to be aware of how to do this for yourself and use your own physiology, thoughts, ideas, sounds, sights and feelings to generate other good feelings, drives and sensations that are going to grow your self-esteem and support you in developing your sense of self.

You can use anchors to capture and re-use positive experiences for yourself to maintain a more progressive state of mind and feelings of well-being. Now have a go at running through this exercise.

Firstly, think of an occasion when you had a highly pleasurable, positive or enjoyable experience. Use your imagination and really immerse yourself in that experience. The best way to do that is to imagine seeing what you saw then (imagine that you are looking out through your own eyes in that situation), hear the sounds that you heard in that experience and feel what you felt then. Think about whereabouts in your body those feelings were and really allow those sensations to be recalled by you. As you feel the sensations increase in intensity as you think and concentrate on them more and more, squeeze the thumb and forefinger of your left hand gently together for a few moments, then release them. Now clear your mind as we did before, maybe by remembering what shoe you put on first today. Then, squeeze your thumb and forefinger together again, gently pulsing them. If you really immersed yourself, that state will return. As you practice and set your mind to it, you can get it to be more and more powerful and stronger and stronger. Use it to anchor all the progressive feelings and sensations that make up your imagined sense of self-esteem and activate it at regular intervals every day.

Another really good thing to do is to enjoy making others feel good around you with this technique. When people enjoy feeling good around you, it is a real tonic for your own self-esteem and self-belief. Identify something that someone you know already does that makes them feel happy or really good about themselves, and create a subtle anchor. Set the anchor while they are doing the activity. Later, fire your anchor and see what happens. If they do the thing you anchored, and you helped them to feel really good again then it worked! This has so many good ramifications for your own self-esteem; it is good to know that others feel good around you.

When you (or someone you are with) are experiencing something you want to have more of, anchor it. Every time you laugh, every time you are complimented and feel good, every time you make someone smile, every time you feel confident just anchor it. Then keep on re-accessing those good experiences for yourself and continue to demonstrate how easy it is for you to feel good and control how you feel when you want to.

As usual, remember that this stuff is powerful so use your new skills wisely. As well, allow yourself to start becoming aware of when it is being used on you, even by people that do not realise they are doing it. Advertisers, politicians and stand-up comedians all know the power of anchors and use them with great cunning. Awareness with anchors is the key – be sure to have fun with them.

Project for today: Set up your own anchor for feeling good about yourself and practice it at least five times a day for the next week.

Day Fifteen

*In the future everybody will be famous for
fifteen minutes.*

Andy Warhol (1968)

Have you ever wondered 'Why am I here?' or 'What am I supposed to do in life?' If so, you are not alone in your thinking. This is one of the most fundamental life decisions you can make and one of the most common questions. Your purpose is about what you plan to achieve and the kind of person you want to be. Your character and your habits will lead you to be healthier, happier and more successful. What are you good at? What do you really enjoy? These are two good places to look when you are trying to decide your direction and we will look at this in more detail as we progress. Your life may well have the potential to be so much more than you might have ever imagined. The most important thing is that your life has meaning for you.

OK, so we are getting on to the climactic big stuff now. Every single person I have met with self-esteem has a sense of purpose about them. A sense of purpose connects with our sense of self in the most fundamental way. For some people it relates to what is beyond their sense of who they are, it is beyond their identity – by that I mean, for some it has more to do with their spirituality. For some, their purpose is at the core of who they are. For others, purpose is the sense of what they value and believe. Once you discover a sense of purpose it enriches you at many levels.

An alternative way of looking at a sense of purpose is to say that it is a sense of meaningfulness, a sense which in turn informs and directs our actions, however large or small, and connects our actions easily to each other. Our purpose also connects our actions to our future in a way that is balanced and congruent with who we are.

I have a great and close friend who left a very well paying job to coach football to children in inner city areas of London. He shared his love of football with the children because he wanted them to have more in their lives. After a couple of years, he became more and more disillusioned, not with the children or their parents or even with the communities that he worked in, but with the system which he saw as perpetuating the problems and providing a cycle of deprivation for them and what he wanted to achieve. The pressure of what he wanted to do began to get the better of him and he realised that he was acting differently towards the children and those colleagues he worked with. He lost his sense of purpose with which he had entered this role and after a couple of extra months, he left his role and went back to his well-paid banking job in the city.

I contrast this to a lady I worked with whose children had left home and husband had retired. Her previous sense of purpose had been on looking after her family and devoting her time and energy and love to her family. She found that she was a little bit lost and did not know what to do with herself; this is something experienced by many. I know of so many people that retire and move to the sea away from family and friends and find themselves lost and without purpose.

Anyway, this lady joined a friend one evening to go to a yoga class and enjoyed it so much that she attended more of them to use up her time and energy. To the surprise of friends and family, she embarked on a teacher training course over a long period of time and set up yoga classes for older people. She became friends with other instructors who took on some of her classes that were getting busier and busier. She ended up writing a best selling book on yoga for older people and went on national and international tours demonstrating her skills and knowledge, something that she had not really known about herself before. She had found a new sense of purpose, and it made her life more meaningful in a variety of ways. She was discovering things about herself that she had not been aware of before which had now given her a sense of independence and identity beyond that which existed before. More importantly for our purposes though; her self-esteem rocketed.

Having some kind of a vision and a sense of purpose is so useful and important if you want to build and develop your growing sense of self-esteem. I am not necessarily saying that you need to know what you want for the rest of your life, of course not, but that you give yourself a sense of purpose. I have a kind of mission statement that came from my early work in these fields. I encountered so many people that had dreams but had no resources, abilities or knowledge of how to achieve those dreams. I vowed to help as many people as I possibly could to achieve their dreams. This still serves as one of my purposes. However, I have other purposes on a daily basis and on a yearly basis that change and become organically different.

There is a notable difference between setting yourself goals to achieve and having a sense of purpose.

- The goals you set yourself have the potential to be achieved. Your purpose is not finite. Your purpose provides the fuel that drives us towards our goals and their achievement.
- Our goals can take us to places we don't want if they do not have a well-formed outcome (you of course do have well-formed outcomes as per our earlier learning!). It is very rare to be misled by a sense of purpose.
- The goals we set ourselves can often fail to live up to what we wanted. Having a sense of purpose is continually rewarding you.
- Goals can create internal conflict. Like when you have a goal of wanting to stop smoking. We want to be healthier, but a part of us likes the time we get to be by ourselves when we smoke. You can often want things in the short term which get in the way of your long term plans. Having a sense of purpose unites all of you and remains harmonious throughout.
- All your goals exist in the future whereas your purpose is an expression of who you are now and who you choose to be now. Your purpose grows out of your past and relates to your present and future.

So What is Your Purpose?

In the 1960s the American psychologist Abraham Maslow made a distinction between 'survival needs' and 'self-actualisation needs'. He also created a hierarchy of needs that is similar to the logical levels that we worked on throughout day two at the beginning of this book. Maslow said that survival needs include food, shelter, warmth – things which if we did not have we might die.

Self-actualisation needs are the things which give our lives meaning: love, challenge, creativity and purpose.

Maslow showed that unless our survival needs are met, of course, we can't begin to notice, let alone satisfy, the self-actualisation needs. The need for a sense of purpose is one of these self-actualisation needs – think about what that means – the idea of self-actualisation. If you have the chance to explore it and to begin working on self-actualisation, you are having your survival needs met and you can really get to work on your self-esteem. What a privilege to be able to have the choice and freedom to explore and develop your own self-esteem. So, survival needs honour and support your purpose. The fact that you have invested in this book suggests that whatever may have happened in the past, you now are looking to focus on self-actualisation.

You see, a sense of purpose goes well beyond achieving the basics in life. The basics are frequently quite solid and specific, whereas purpose is abstract and more inclusive. Wanting to have a new car is a goal: being able to travel freely with a sense of independence may well be a means to a purpose. Travelling might mean being able to enlarge your horizons and have more experience by which to serve your fellow man for example.

Having a sense of purpose is something which agrees with you and your life at all levels. A goal may well fit with a part of you, but not with another. Goals can provoke internal conflict, purpose cannot. Your purpose may evolve or change the way it seeks to express itself; but it does not run out. Remember my friend who wanted to coach under privileged children? He eventually retrained as a hypnotherapist and set up a private practice and it was with me that he trained; thus we became friends. He learnt how to help others and he also specialised in working with children. His purpose had not changed; he just found a way that allowed him to express it more easily and freely.

Finding Purpose

Your sense of purpose is likely to be driven by your beliefs and values. Therefore, it is also likely to include many aspects of your own identity; it may even go well beyond that. I have met people who have known what their purpose in life is since they were young. I would say that most people discover their purpose as they go along. If your purpose seems to be hidden, you might want to reflect on the patterns of your life so far.

Have a think about the issues that you have been most concerned with. What gets you most excited in life? What are your values that you promote or defend? What really matters to you? We have seen already how patterned our behaviours and thinking can be. However unconscious or subtle your life purpose may be, it may well have been informing us and guiding us all along and throughout our life.

The illness of someone very close to me as well as lots of issues of my own in earlier life led me to discover hypnosis and personal development and that in turn led me to do vastly different things with my life, though these things have been different, my underlying purpose has been similar and has been honoured in many different ways. I love that. My work now goes beyond meeting people and training; it goes into books, articles, audio programmes all over the world and none of it would have been possible if I had not had an underlying purpose propelling it.

I consider myself very fortunate to have discovered a sense of purpose. I have also been fortunate to have discovered the tools that I needed to put my sense of purpose into action and all those tools that I have used are here within this book to be shared and applied by others. So, what if you have not yet found your sense of purpose? This is true of many, many people, so let's look at how to go about finding some sense of purpose.

It has been my experience that people who cannot discover their purpose have not learnt to value or tune into themselves. Many people even associate and confuse self-awareness with 'selfishness', and self-consideration with 'self-absorption'. If you happen to be one of those people, then an important initial step to take in finding your life purpose may well be to deal with these beliefs and the personal history that developed those beliefs. This does not mean ignoring your past and any connection to it, because you learnt a lot from your past, despite my views about analysing it too much. We are all amazing learning machines, we just continue to learn and learn. Much of what we consider to be usual about ourselves are things that we have had to learn and they can pretty much all be changed or 'un-learnt'.

We are going to look at identifying and letting go of any limiting beliefs later in the book, however, we can continue to learn from our past without being made a slave to past conditioning. If you are thinking that you have been limiting yourself in this way or you are thinking that you have always been a certain way and therefore you simply must stay that way forever, then keep on using the techniques in this book, develop them and tailor them to yourself. You can break previous programming with persistent new thought and investing of your energy into yourself. Life continues to show us more and more opportunities to explore and exercise our life's purpose. It has been my experience that when we actually start looking and noticing and being aware of ourselves, our purpose is usually there.

Project for today: Write down your answers to these questions as thoroughly as possible with as much detail and exploration as you can.

- What are you passionate about? What pushes your buttons or turns you on?
- What is it about this that gets you so involved?
- As you think about one of the things that you are passionate about, answer this; what does it do for you? Regardless of how unusual the answer to this may be, really take note of it and ask yourself 'What does that do for me?' When you have answered that question, ask it again of your answer 'and what does that do for me?' then whatever you answer, keep asking that question until you cannot ask it anymore. What you are doing is asking what the purpose is behind it and you get more and more significant answers as you keep asking the question. When you get to the stage where you can't ask the question any further, you have discovered the purpose behind your passion.
- What did you love as a child? Is it still important to you? Again, ask yourself the questions from the previous one to get your purpose behind that thing. Is that purpose still valid? Has it changed? Have you lost touch with it somehow?

As I have encouraged you to do throughout this book, really do this, answer thoroughly and with meaning and honesty. Then as the person who knows you best, decide on a plan of action to take and think about what you need to do next in establishing a sense of purpose.

Day Sixteen

*She was only sixteen, only sixteen, and I was
too young to know.*

Dr Hook, *Only Sixteen*

Having enhanced self-esteem had a truly magical impact on my life, you know what though; the real magic is that it can be created. You can create magic in your life. Each day offers up new and exciting opportunities to strengthen your sense of self. The real magic is learning to like yourself more, to learn how to manage your states and how to discover and realise your sense of purpose.

This book has focussed on how to strengthen your sense of self, how to like yourself more and more, how to manage and develop your states and how to discover your life purpose. Go back over the various days learnings and projects and listen again and again to really get a sense of all these elements, I guarantee that you will discover things that you may have missed first time around. Trust yourself when you encounter things that have not been discussed in this book, enhancing your self-esteem to supreme levels is an ongoing process, not because we never get there but because there are always more opportunities for becoming a more developed, more rounded, successful and happy human being. Testing and trusting the information that you give yourself and derive from your own senses and experiences is simply the best way to make your journey more progressive and fulfilling.

Now that you are developing your self-esteem, let's also progress onto boosting some confidence:

Confidence Enhancement

At the time of writing this book, it is the build up to the 2006 World Cup Football finals being held in Germany. Due to my love of football, I have been keenly listening to the pre-match banter and talk surrounding the upcoming fixtures, and the displayed levels of confidence inherent in the England camp are quite unlike previous years. So, as I am going to write about confidence today, I want to start with some basic stuff and move on to some really powerful techniques. The reason that I mention the football is that when someone is confident, they seem to perform better and the England football team seem to be playing better and better at the moment which runs parallel to their growing confidence.

Before you proceed and I go into any further detail, I want you to think about this notion; even though one of my audio products is titled 'Think Yourself Thin', you cannot 'think' yourself anything. Otherwise, you would all just think about pots of gold arriving in your front rooms and you would all be rich (or whatever your interpretation of wealth and success is). However, the pots of gold do not arrive just by thinking about them. Something needs to be done to get them. It is good to be open to receiving life's abundance, but it won't just appear.

When anyone is developing a new behaviour of any kind, enhancing their confidence or updating their current behaviours in any way at all, there needs to be an element of action that is taken to alter things properly. Something new needs to be done enough times for the unconscious mind to learn it.

The early 'success philosophers' and gurus like Stephen Covey and Napoleon Hill recognised that in order for a new behaviour to happen unconsciously and automatically, it needs to be done for 21 consecutive days. So then the new behaviour is learnt thoroughly by the unconscious mind and can begin to let it happen on auto-pilot. The new behaviours can then happen without you having to think about them.

So, any new behaviour needs some conscious effort and repeated application to happen unconsciously. That is the reason that I continue to adopt the school teacher style nagging about completing the projects each day; I want to ensure that you take action to get your brain doing new things.

Now, when you have a new way of doing things, the other, old, unwanted way of doing things doesn't just wither away instantly. It remains in the bank so to speak. If you were confined to a wheelchair, the muscles in your legs would begin to experience wheelchair, the muscles in your legs would begin to experience atrophy due to them not being used, the same way that when certain parts of your brain are not used, they experience a similar kind atrophy. This is why it is difficult for us to learn languages when we are much older and school kids find it a bit easier; that part of our brain has not been used for a long time.

The old behaviour needs significant time to experience atrophy.

Imagine that here and now as you read this, your unconscious mind has carved out a distinct pathway of behaviour and this pathway is well defined. Every time you enter certain situations or circumstances, your unconscious mind carries on down that well trodden pathway that you have always gone down. It is the only way that it knows and it is the easiest route to take.

When you create an alternative, new behaviour, a desired confident behaviour, you are carving out a new pathway that needs to be trodden down well, several times, so that your unconscious knows it is there and knows that it can take this route in certain circumstances, events and situations.

OK. So then, by repeatedly taking the new pathway, the old pathway can begin to overgrow and have its own atrophy. However, we all know how easy it is to unearth an old pathway. If we allow ourselves to go back along that way it can begin to get carved out again.

These notions can form the foundation of any programme of change that you embark upon. I find this true when people invest in the hypnotic audio programmes that I have created. So many people think that all they need is to be hypnotised by the recording and then 'shazam', changes will occur without having to do anything and Adam the magician hypnotist has worked his magic spell on you. If only such a thing could happen! The changes are lodged inside, but they need motion and require stimulating into action.

So, we now know that we need to get some changes going consciously in order to get them communicated to the unconscious part of us. Now you can throw yourself into these exercises and techniques knowing that they need consistent application to help boost your confidence.

So, let's proceed on to the fun stuff.

Learn to Love That Person in the Mirror

When we have received enough love in our life and really felt the love we have been given, it teaches us that we are valuable. Even if we happen to get something wrong, or make a mistake or two, we are still valuable and important. Inside of yourself, you know that you are a good idea.

It is that notion that is one of the keys to happiness and a deep rooted self-confidence. Deep inside you know that you are valuable, so when you need to feel more confident, you can remember that just being you is always good enough. However, I am sure that all of you, like so many of us, have experienced things that cause us to forget that and lead us to seek our sense of value from outside ourselves.

So in order to feel confident when we are out in the world, the consumer culture all around us offers us ways to buy self-confidence by buying those shoes, that coat, that car, the house with the swimming pool, and so on. I know people that feel differently about having bought the right brands too! We have associations and emotional attachments to certain brands that trigger responses within us.

There was a time in my life when if I ever felt tired or worn out, I would drink green tea. This would perk me up, I even had to have a certain brand whose packaging style I liked and advertising had resonated well with me. However, I now know that if I am really tired, then I can use some self hypnosis, or have a lie down, or just rest in some quiet for a while to replenish my energy.

The problem is that brands do for self-confidence what green tea does for relaxation. They substitute an external source of good feeling for your natural internal one. Then in the longer term, borrowing your good feelings from elsewhere prevents you developing your own natural inner resources.

It is better to replenish your self-confidence from the inside than to borrow your good feelings from a brand.

Some people even borrow their good feelings from someone else. Have you ever met a psychic vampire or people that seem to suck and drain the fun out of things? Or someone who only feels good about themselves when they are with another person to use and feed off their self-confidence?

When I first became involved with the world of hypnosis and personal development, I read a wonderful book by a man called Dr Maxwell Maltz entitled *Psycho Cybernetics* that formed the basis of lots of the techniques that we have used already in this book and many modern ideas as to how we understand personalities.

Dr Maltz was a plastic surgeon and he found that if he changed the way people looked, it often changed their personality too. When people looked different, they also felt different. Often people that had initially lacked confidence were transformed into more confident, outgoing people who lived life with more vigour and passion following their surgery.

What perplexed Dr Maltz is that some of his clients did not seem to get happier. Some, whose appearance had changed a lot, didn't seem to change their feelings. They still felt lacking in confidence.

So what Dr Maltz concluded was that cosmetic surgery would not benefit the client if they had a poor image of themselves. His solution was to create a visualisation technique that helped them to change their inner self-image. He had some wonderful results. So when the clients changed the way they felt about themselves, they became happier and more fulfilled and their confidence grew. The technique is like many that I have shown before, however, here it is in its simplest form.

Firstly, imagine yourself as you would ideally like to be. Think about how you would look if you were as happy and confident as you wanted to be. How do you walk? What do you wear? What expressions are on your face? Where do you go? Take all the time necessary for this, to really get an idea of how you are when you are confident with yourself.

Secondly, when you know what you will look like, make a film clip inside your mind, in your imagination of yourself being happy, confident and deeply self-assured.

Thirdly, imagine yourself stepping into that film, imagine seeing through those eyes, hearing through those ears, and feel those confident feelings, think to yourself; 'How do I know the confident feelings? Where in my body are they?' Enjoy feeling and being exactly how you want to be.

Lastly for this exercise, imagine that when you get up tomorrow you awaken as that ideal you, feeling this good and imagine the day going as you want it to.

Your Sense of Self

Your sense of who you are and who you perceive yourself to be, that is, your self-image, often works like a self-fulfilling prophecy. Remember I said in one of those early days that what you believe to be the truth is the truth for you? One of my oldest and best friends will not mind me saying that he is unlikely to be getting his face onto the cover of any magazines, I mean he is not typically good looking (whatever that might be) however, he thinks of himself as attractive, he has a sense of self that he believes in and as a result he has a certain manner and a way about him that people are attracted to. Therefore you can see that anyone who truly believes and accepts themselves as being a certain way; unattractive or lacking in self-confidence and self-esteem for example, are simply sabotaging their chances of being anything other than that.

So, your self-image and what you allow yourself to believe about yourself is a very important element to be aware of here. Remember, you can never be better on the outside than you believe yourself to be on the inside. Your internal state is very much physiologically represented on the outside; it is then transmitted to every one via that massive antenna that you have too!

How you allow yourself to think about and perceive yourself also affects how other people feel about you. Other people are constantly responding to your non-verbal communication and your body language even without consciously knowing they are doing so. The tone of your voice, your manner and your emotional signals are all transmitting messages about how you feel about yourself. If you are lacking confidence, you can say all the confident words in the world but you are sure to be demonstrating non-confident body language and other signals.

As much as you sometimes might wish it to be true, no other person can actually reach inside of us and alter our feelings for us. If you really want to feel more confident, your self-image needs to be updated and enhanced. If you think of yourself as successful, warm and confident, you can enter any situation with your head held high, standing tall and feeling safe and protected by it. You are feeling good about yourself and that feeling allows you a sense of boldness and protection.

People all tend to react on auto-pilot to life according to their relationships with themselves. Your self-image is your inner sense of yourself and you refer to that part of yourselves all the time to unconsciously work out how to behave, act or react in certain events and circumstances. In other words, your reactions are founded in your self-image and sense of self.

Therefore, creating, enhancing and increasing a progressive, positive self-image ensures that your automatic reactions come from a sense of freedom and confidence and are powerful. They do not come from a place of fear or limitation. These last four paragraphs are among the most important I have ever written – if you want to be more confident, read them over again.

Mirroring Confidence

I once attended a training course with Michael Breen and the famous Paul Mckenna. Michael Breen had devised a wonderful technique that I use a lot with many of the individual clients that consult with me. The reason I like it so much is because it makes you instantly feel good about yourself. It gives you a tangible way of demonstrating to yourself that you can be in charge of your feelings through your thoughts. This simple technique can be done absolutely any time that you are in a room with a mirror.

So many people go through life conditioning themselves to feel uncomfortable or bad when they look into a mirror. They do this by looking into it and thinking about fat, wrinkles, a blemish or by noticing a spot! I have noticed several of my friends look into a mirror and 'tut' at themselves while reminding themselves of all the things that attack their confidence and diminish their sense of self. So this technique interrupts that process and allows you to recondition yourself to feel better and more confident about being you.

OK, so first up, take a seat or position yourself comfortably in view of a mirror so that you will be able to see your entire self, however, do not look into it straight away. Just wait and look away for a moment. Have a nice clear mind; maybe think about the colour white for a few seconds.

Secondly then, think about an occasion when someone you know was being sincere when they paid you a compliment. Think of anything, however innocuous it may seem, it can be any compliment what so ever of any kind. Remember it.

Thirdly, remember what it was that they said and hear it again in your mind and remember how it made you feel. Locate where in your body those feelings were. Really tune into them.

Fourthly, imagine that feeling of being complimented, loved and cherished spreading through your system. You can even imagine giving it a colour as it is working it's way into your cells and into your mind. Really imagine it spreading and travelling through you. Imagine that the more it spreads, the more intense the feelings become. Double your feelings and concentrate on them growing and feeling better and better. Create as much inner joy and good feeling as you possibly can right now.

Now, turn or look up and into the mirror. Really look at yourself while feeling that feeling. Allow your mind to make a distinct connection and a deep association with that feeling and your mirror reflection. Spend some time enjoying this feeling and really focusing on the image of yourself.

Finally, imagine taking a picture in your mind with an imaginary camera of yourself just like the image you see in the mirror. Then imagine putting that picture right into the centre of your heart. Deliver that picture and all the new associated feelings to your heart. Keep it there, hold it right there, so that you can look at it and feel it whenever you want to remind yourself of how good you can feel.

Lots of people that have used my *Ultimate Confidence* audio programme, those that have worked with me individually or attended personal development seminars of mine often say to me that they are worried that this increase in confidence might be short term. They worry that they may well drift back to being the old version of themselves again soon. Some people worry that the confidence does not feel real or genuine, in fact it feels insincere. In order to reassure those people, I tell them two things.

I have said it before and I will say it again now. You deserve to feel increasingly more and more wonderful about yourself every day. It is your birthright to feel however you want to feel. You deserve this, it is your birthright.

Secondly, your sense of confidence in yourself is innate, it is inherent within you. It is part of us all and you possess it from birth. Lots of people can and do often lose touch with their confidence and for a variety of reasons they learn to worry or reduce their confidence. However, confidence is simply hard-wired into your brain. It does always exist there beneath your worries or limiting beliefs and stresses. Fears, worries, anxiety and any sense of lack are all things that can increase and decrease, and they can be learnt and unlearnt. Your confidence is always there beneath all that.

It is like when a baby keeps on wanting to walk and keeps on falling down and keeps on at it. However many times they stumble, they get up and they learn and they benefit from it. The persistence is rewarded. Your confidence is hard-wired into you. We all have it. Every aspect of this day's learning are ways of reminding you of what you already have.

As I said when I opened up on this day's learning. When you have received enough love in your life and really felt the love you have been given, it teaches you that you are valuable. That love can come from yourself and does not have to come from any external source. As you follow these exercises and develop the right self-image it leads to you knowing deep inside of yourself, that you are a good idea.

Project for today: Run through the first exercise and spend some time acting as if you were the confident person that you know you want to be now. Also do the second exercise looking into a mirror.

Day Seventeen

I kissed her slender hand,
She took the kiss sedately;
Maud is not seventeen,
But she is tall and stately.

Lord Alfred Tennyson, *Maud* (1855)

OK, OK, so I admit it, this year I have watched one or two episodes of Celebrity Big Brother on the TV here in the UK. I am not a reality game show fanatic, however, I find them fascinating, absolutely fascinating.

One thing that I have found fascinating is how different people react to others just because of what they believed before they entered the house rather than treating individuals on the basis of how they have experienced them first hand.

There was a young musician in the Big Brother house called Preston. He voted for a lady called Faria to be evicted from the house simply because of the fact that she is famous for a 'kiss and tell' story with England football coach Sven Goran Erickson. The first evictee, Jodie Marsh, was also cold and unpleasant to Faria on the first night for the very same reason and expressed that thought to Dennis Rodman who was also in the house. Yet neither of them judged Faria on how they found her or on their own personal experience of her.

Jodie and Preston both openly stated the belief that they thought she was not a 'proper celebrity' (whatever that is) because of how she became famous. Jodie Marsh actually said, when she was evicted from the house in the first week, that she thought Faria was lovely! Amazing stuff, albeit very contradictory to what she had previously been saying. When Jodie got to know Faria beyond what she originally believed, she discovered something that was liberating and kind instead of to the contrary.

Oh how our limiting beliefs make us act! How people's beliefs limit them! How wonderful it is when we change limiting beliefs, eh? Imagine how your beliefs about yourself affect your self-esteem and sense of self.

Your beliefs are pretty much the rules of your life, well at least they are the rules that you will no doubt be living by. These rules may be what sets you free to achieve things in your life and live the way that you think is important. These beliefs may well also be restricting you and holding you back. They may even be creating the belief that you are incapable of achieving your goals. Or as in the case of contestants from Celebrity Big Brother, stop you from being agreeable to someone.

Your beliefs may well be affecting your degree of success with enhancing your self-esteem.

I believe in gravity and I am guessing that you all believe in it too. Now, I have never been inclined to test gravity by trying to walk on air as that would be crazy. Gravity is not influenced or altered in any way, shape or form by my belief in it or yours for that matter. However, our relationships, abilities, possibilities and sense of self are all influenced by our beliefs about them and resulting attitudes towards them.

We mostly tend to form our beliefs as the result of our experiences and then we act as if they are true. Like so many other aspects of this book, in one sense they are self-fulfilling prophecies. If you believe that you are a likeable person, you will act that way, approach people openly, be agreeable, warm and enjoy being with people. They will warm to you and so confirm your belief. This builds self-esteem. We think that beliefs are formed by experiences, but equally experiences are the results of beliefs. Hmm. Interesting stuff eh?

So this then means that you can choose your beliefs. Which is another thing that I get excited by.

Before we all start getting too excited at this prospect (I can tell that you are all on the edge of your seats now), understand that the belief that beliefs are changeable is in itself a challenging belief to many people because they tend to think of beliefs as possessions. People talk about 'holding' and 'having' beliefs, 'losing' or 'gaining' them. No one wants to 'lose' something. It would be better talking about them 'leaving' or 'outgrowing' beliefs rather than 'losing' them.

In addition to that, we all have a personal investment in our own beliefs. We have invested valuable thought and energy into our beliefs and it takes us a lot to budge them. If the world or life ever confirms them, then they make a lot of sense to us. They are then predictable and give us a sense of security and certainty. We even may take a perverse pleasure in disaster, providing we have predicted it. How many of you have used the term 'I told you so' and found it to be a satisfying phrase? Not because you necessarily wanted anything to go wrong, but because your beliefs were proved correct.

So, let me move on to the subject of negative and limiting beliefs.

Limiting beliefs are the major offender stopping us from achieving our goals and living our dreams and enjoying a deep sense of self-esteem. Limiting beliefs act as rules that stop us from getting what exists within us as potential. We all have so much potential but we do not tap into it nearly enough. Limiting beliefs hold us back from achieving what we are actually capable of and what we deserve.

So have a good think about this question. What is stopping you from having good levels of self-esteem or confidence? Right now it is important to realise and know that the answers are often your limiting beliefs.

Early limiting beliefs may come from childhood influences such as parents or teachers or people whose beliefs we deemed worthy of believing ourselves. These early beliefs often stay hidden and we do not consciously evaluate them as adults. We also pick up limiting beliefs from the media. The numerous soap operas that take up so many hours of TV time set up situations where the characters have to act out ridiculous limitations; otherwise there simply is no drama to compulsively view!

Here are some typical limiting beliefs that are amazingly common:

'I need to have lots of money to be happy or show that I am successful.'

'I can't trust myself in certain situations.'

'I have always lacked self-esteem, so I always will.'

'You can't get over a bad start in life.'

'I am too old to learn to learn how to feel good about myself.'

'I can't feel good about myself without other people feeling bad about themselves.'

'I never get what I am after.'

'Other people are better than me.'

'I do not deserve to be successful.'

'I can't get what I want.'

'I have reached my limits.'

'I need to work very hard to have enough money to live.'

'Success takes a very long time.'

This is important. These and similar beliefs are only true if you act as if they are. Suppose your beliefs are mistaken? What difference would that make? Is the difference worthwhile? Are you harbouring any limiting beliefs about yourself and your own sense of self? Well are you? Investigate and examine this.

In the process of achieving increased self-esteem and confidence, sometimes just being able to articulate limiting beliefs can dismantle them. Highlight and exposing any old, unwanted limiting beliefs and noticing their effect is often enough to alter or dissolve and dissipate them, therefore changing and updating your own reality.

It has certainly been my experience that the majority of people are not usually aware of their limiting beliefs. Especially limiting beliefs about themselves. So the first step is to put them into language by writing them down. Get them down in writing in that journal of yours. Then they are exposed and can be examined and ideally let go of. There are two simple ways to do this.

The first way, as mentioned previously, is to simply ask yourself what the reasons are that you are not currently experiencing the amazing levels of self-esteem that you want to. What do you think is holding you back? Ask yourself that question and answer as truthfully and thoroughly as you can. The answers will reveal what it is that you perceive to be your limitations. More often than not, these limits will be more about you than about the world. When they are about you, they are something that can be changed or updated.

A good principle to work from is the following: Whatever you say is preventing you from achieving your goal is a belief and comes from you, not from reality.

Barriers to success are created in the outside world from limiting beliefs in your mind. Now, I have found that when people do ask themselves these questions (as mentioned earlier) in their own mind, they are rarely honest with themselves. Here is another approach that I use a lot with my one to one clients to discover what, if any, limiting beliefs they have.

Firstly, as you think about that idea of increasing your self-esteem to the levels that you want in your life, the levels that will revolutionise your life, assess and score each of the following statements:

Score each of these statements by giving them a score out of 10. Where one means you do not believe this statement and ten means that you believe it without a doubt at all.

- I deserve to have high self-esteem.
- I have the skills and abilities necessary to develop my self-esteem.
- It is possible for me to increase my self-esteem.
- The way for me to increase my self-esteem is clear and defined.
- Having increased self-esteem is desirable to me.
- Enhanced and increased self-esteem is worthwhile.

Look at the scores that you have written down and look at the lowest scores for any of your answers and begin to explore them. This can be wonderfully enlightening. Low scores highlight and indicate a possible limiting belief. If you have discovered some doubts in some areas, now begin to ask yourself about the reasons you are doubtful or what could be making you doubt this statement? List and write down your answers.

When you begin to question and examine your beliefs you can unearth what might be limiting beliefs. Then you can begin to heighten your awareness of whether or not your beliefs are preventing you from achieving your goals.

Changing Beliefs

I have to admit it, this year I became addicted to watching the wonderful TV series 'Lost'. For me, it has been the best thing on television for a good few years now. It reminded me how I was when Twin Peaks was going strong all those years ago when I was younger. So I recently got hold of the first series of Twin Peaks and watched it again recently. I have now seen those shows many times and as with 'Lost' I still have no idea what the heck is going on!

Now, as a man with a wild and vivid imagination, I have entered all manner of debates with friends, family and colleagues about what is going on in the TV show 'Lost', about what they think and what we believe about it all. I have been finding myself in a similar state as when I was a child, being easily led into all kinds of naughty shenanigans by others. Whenever some one tells me their theory, I change my mind about what is going on in 'Lost'.

I have had tales from people telling me that they have friends who know the director of 'Lost' and have told me what their theory was and so on and so forth. Each time someone has given me a good reason or a great thought, my brain has gone into overdrive and my beliefs about my theory have changed.

So having identified any limiting beliefs, I now want to progress onto how you go about changing and updating limiting beliefs and changing some of your big life beliefs about yourself as easily as if you were changing your beliefs about a TV show.

So here we go with the belief changing process. The first step in our belief changing process is to do that which you have just done; identify the limiting belief that you have about yourself that you want to shift.

Having identified a belief that you think is limiting or restrictive or causing you problems, make sure that you write it down concisely and precisely. When you get a belief down on paper and look at it in that way (I am not suggesting that you pull faces at the words by the way!) it then begins to dissipate. It is exposed and vulnerable. You should have done this already and written down your identified limited belief.

The next step is to look at that written limiting belief, think about it and ask yourself what it is doing for you; how do you benefit from having that belief about yourself? I know it is a strange question, but ask yourself it anyway. What purpose is that belief serving; this must be something positive, keep asking yourself what the positive intention is of that belief. Believe me when I say that there is one; otherwise you would not have this belief, would you?

Regardless of the fact that it may be limiting you and hindering your self-esteem development in a variety of ways, there is a positive intention behind every limiting belief. There is a way in which you benefit from having that belief and now is the time to find that out; find out what purpose it is serving.

The third step then is to now ask yourself what you would prefer to believe instead. What would you rather believe about yourself?

Then guess what I am going to ask you to do? You guessed right, well done. Write it down. Of course, there are some rules about this new desired belief. Firstly, it has to be stated positively and progressively, remember that you want to move towards what you want to believe about yourself, not move away from what you do not want to believe about yourself. Ask for what you want, not what you don't want to believe.

Secondly, you must ensure that you are comfortable and happy with the desired belief, make sure that it does not harm, conflict with or upset anyone to have this belief; that includes yourself!

Thirdly, it needs to satisfy the same positive intention as you discovered that the old belief had.

So, go ahead and write down this new belief about yourself. Also, make sure that it is worded in the present tense, by that I mean phrase it as if it is occurring now. For example if your goal were to achieve your ideal weight, a suitable new belief would be, 'I am believing increasingly more in my ability to achieve my ideal weight'.

By doing that now, you have made the desired belief relevant and pertinent and you have gone and given it flow, direction and energy. Get it worded in the present tense and move on to the next step.

The fourth step in this wonderful process is to recall a time when you doubted a belief.

Can you remember an occasion when you doubted something that you really used to hold as a firm belief? You may wish to reflect on your life. Think about the kind of beliefs that you had at certain times in your life, I know that mine have changed and altered a great deal over the years. I remember having solid beliefs about certain things when I was at college and can remember doubting those beliefs as I learnt more about life and throughout my studies at university.

When you think about that period of doubt, how did you know that you doubted your belief? Did you have certain sensations in your body? What were you thinking about? How did you think about it? What were you experiencing? Really see if you can get back into that state of doubt, psychologically and physiologically.

While in that state, bring to the forefront of your mind the old unwanted limiting belief that you identified earlier and have a think about your old limiting belief that you want to shed. Do this while in that doubting state.

Great isn't it? Who would have thought that there are advantages to doubting things?

So, as you do this, begin picking away at the old withering belief by asking yourself:

'What are the disadvantages of this old belief?'

'Does it really fit in with what is truly important in my life?'

'In the past, when was having this old belief getting in the way of my success?'

'What would it be like to not have this old belief?'

Before moving on to the next step, take a breather. When you sit down to run through this process, take a couple of minutes out now, think of something completely different; what shoe did you put on first when you went to work this morning? What do I really think is going on in 'Lost?'

The fifth step requires a similar process to previous steps, however, as you think back through your life, just have a think about times when you have been impressionable, willing to learn, open to change and especially open to new beliefs. Remember everything about that wonderful state of receptivity. How did it feel? Where in your body were the feelings? What did you see? What internal dialogue did you have? Really run through as much as you possibly can to achieve that state again for yourself right now?

As you recall a time when you were open to a new belief, really focus on and think about your new desired belief while in this open, receptive state. Now ask yourself:

'How would it feel to have your desired belief?'

'How is it a better belief than the old one?'

'What difference would it make to your life to have this new belief?'

'What things would you do that you have not been doing?'

'What would you be able to achieve and overcome now?'

To round off this step nicely, take some time out now to evaluate the new belief. How good does it feel? Is there any tweaking to do? Can you make it even better and even more empowering?

The sixth step is about relaxing.

Get yourself nice and relaxed and breathing deeply and comfortably and then go ahead and imagine that deep inside of you exists a large furnace. If you really want to be free of the old belief forever, then imagine tossing it into the furnace and watch it burn away to nothing.

The final step is all about taking some action. Make a choice to take some action. What can you and what will you do differently this very day as a result of having this wonderful new belief about yourself? How about you set yourself a task, to achieve today, a task that is based on this new belief being true for you and your life now. Something that represents and demonstrates how happy you are with yourself. Start doing things differently straight away and get that new belief firmly embedded into your unconscious behaviour patterns. When you start to do things differently, you then have physiological support and experience of the new belief and it becomes verified and enhanced with each new day. This is practically applying self-esteem to your life.

Changing your beliefs can actually be as simple as passing beliefs about a television programme that you follow. To change them powerfully and mindfully requires some continued concentration and requires a good investment of time and energy. However, when you do change, update and upgrade your beliefs, this can and does subsequently open the way for a major change in your experience of life and a rapid progression towards successfully achieving your goals and enriching your experience of life.

Enjoy this process, have some fun with it and get to the heart of your own development with updating any outmoded beliefs.

Project for today: Identify and expose any limiting beliefs that relate to your self-esteem or confidence. Then go about changing them into your desired beliefs by running through the previous process.

Day Eighteen

Common sense is nothing more than a deposit of prejudices laid down in the mind before you reach eighteen.

Albert Einstein cited in
The Universe and Dr Einstein (1950)

Protecting Yourself from Things That Used to Damage Your Self-Esteem

At the time of writing this, I have just been on the filming set of a new BBC1 primetime TV series called 'Run For Glory'. The programme charts 13 people who have amazingly valiant reasons for wanting to raise money for charity by running the London Marathon. The participants range from a 26 year old man who has been HIV positive since he was 18, a mother whose son is terminally ill, a man whose son committed suicide and a lady with suspected terminal cancer who has battled against cancer for years. They all have wonderful reasons for raising this money. None of them were runners before this show and they are being trained by UK Olympic gold medallists Steve Cram and Sally Gunnell. I have been filming for one of the shows to help them overcome psychological barriers and get in control of their minds with regards to running the marathon and their preparation.

I found it very interesting to observe the relations between the crew, the producers and the interactions with and in between the participants of the show and how other people really do affect each other and have an impact on each other. Some of the slightest things affect how others behave and someone who at one stage seems quite sure of themselves is suddenly quiet and meek.

When I was much younger, I worked for a central London company. I had been out the night before, had a very late night and had overslept and had to rush to work in a state of poor preparation. I had a huge crush on the girl who worked as the company receptionist, I mean she was gorgeous! She should have been a model. Every day when I walked past her, I would try and be cool and witty and usually acted in such a way that made me look foolish. Anyway, I walked in following this late night and this beautiful receptionist, girl of my dreams, said to me 'Ooh Adam, you look terrible today'. She meant nothing by it, however, I felt as though someone had struck my heart with an axe. I spent the entire day hiding away and feeling dreadful about myself. She had confirmed that I had nothing to offer anyone in the entire world ever. I really got things out of perspective. If only I had known how to protect myself and known how to not allow certain things to affect me as they once did.

One of the things that I have noticed since I started working within the various fields of personal development is that I am much more aware of other people and how I interact with them.

I have practised and practised achieving a really enjoyable sense of rapport with people when I meet them and develop relationships with them. It has been great to observe my own improvements in how I do this and the kind of intuitive and instinctive way that I do this. As your self-esteem grows you will notice how much easier it is for you to do this too and it is sure to happen. There is something to beware of here though.

When working on the set of this TV show, I was chatting to one of the participants who is about to become very famous here in the UK thanks to this TV show. They were telling me that at the end of these filming days, despite all the good things they were learning and achieving with the others, with everything going really well, they would finish the day feeling drained and verging on being depressed and felt really bad about themselves.

I spoke to them for a while and I was not sure about this until I observed all the kinds of interaction that was there in this unusual TV environment – the participant was getting excellent results. I mean they are doing so amazingly well, so why were they feeling so low? They should have been feeling amazing about themselves, especially at having achieved so much.

I suggested that this person might be picking up other people's issues, thoughts and feelings. Others were maybe affecting her. I suggested that maybe she needed to protect herself. She used the technique that I then demonstrated to her and subsequently reported back that she felt amazing. She felt so much better than she did before when she was around these people that were stressed, having great demands placed upon them and facing some very challenging situations in their lives. She was able to not allow these other people to affect her sense of self and it was a joy for her.

When you develop rapport with people and get close to them, especially when you are growing in confidence, it can get knocked and send you back to a place near to where you began. This happens because you can and often do access some of what the other people are thinking and feeling. While this can be very useful, it is not the best news when the person you are matching is not in a great or a productive state with low self-esteem themselves.

It is like a friend of mine who I joke is a 'fun vampire'. Sometimes he is so morose and seemingly depressed when we are out socially that he seems to 'suck the life and the fun' out of all the people that he encounters! I know you know someone like that too.

I tend to find this is particularly important when I am running seminars with people that are making a lot of changes in their lives or if I am working therapeutically with individuals. I want to be sure not to take on board too much of their feelings and way of thinking. So I want to show you some ways of protecting yourself too, so that your confidence and self-esteem are not dented by others and you can step out boldly into the world knowing that your developing self-esteem is invincible.

The way I suggest of doing this requires your natural ability to use your imagination and visualise. Now, if you believe you have difficulty visualising or using your imagination, trust me when I tell you that you use your imagination every day. Your imagination is what reminds you what your partner or spouse looks like, what colour your front door is and how your childhood bedroom looked. You do not have to be visualising in perfect cinema screen pictures in your mind, just do it in a way that is right for you. This method is just as effective if you visualise the things I ask or if you just pretend to visualise them in your mind.

Firstly, get yourself nice and relaxed. Sit still and take some longer, deeper breaths and then allow your breathing to be natural and become rhythmic and easy. Focus on the moment; be aware of how your body feels in that moment.

Secondly, as you get more relaxed, imagine the relaxation spreading through your body. If you want to, give it a colour or a texture or imagine it as a sensation.

Thirdly, imagine the relaxation, or the sensation of stillness moving out of your body, just a few centimetres. Imagine that you are extending it to become a protective shield that is all around you.

Imagine that it acts as a filter, so you only to take on board the things that are for your better good and understanding. Make sure the filter stops anything that is going to affect your self-esteem detrimentally from being allowed into your mind.

I don't know if you will remember adverts for the oat cereal Ready Brek? The people used to have a glow about them when they were going to work if they had eaten their Ready Brek. When I first started protecting myself in this wonderful way, I used to imagine that I had a glow around me that acted like emotional armour and any unwanted thoughts or feelings or even comments from others that I did not want to carry around with me just bounced off my armour.

Finally, when relaxing tell yourself that this protective shield is there working for you even if you are not consciously aware of it. That way you can be sure that you are not carrying anyone else's vibes around with you, this leaves you free to enjoy your experiences for what they really are. Your self-esteem stays intact or it continues to grow safe in the knowledge that you are in control of your mind and protecting yourself from outside influences. Then go ahead and practice this a few times, putting conscious effort into it, imagine making it more powerful with your attention and really getting it strong.

These ideas are just metaphors for protecting yourself, but because your mind and body are one system, they can be extremely effective ways of letting your unconscious know what you want. One of the things that you may begin to notice after you have used this approach a few times and over a prolonged period of time is that you just need to remind yourself of it every now and then. Then it works even better and better. The long term effects of establishing some protection are so very good for you; just as good as finding a good sun screen, that's for sure.

One of the things you may discover is how many people out there make negative or bad suggestions (i.e. people who say things which guide attention in less than helpful directions). The number of well-meaning doctors, family members, colleagues and friends that I have heard giving people suggestions for ill health, stress and negativity is truly amazing! If you maintain some good protection for yourself, you can be sure not to allow other peoples negative language, thoughts and feelings to affect you in a way that is not for the better good of your self-esteem.

The ability to protect myself from the things going on around me has been instrumental in my latter life, being able to block out most unhelpful messages that come my way leaves a very nice state of well-being.

Project for today: Run yourself through this process and really concentrate on installing your own protective shield.

Day Nineteen

One of the things that has been inherent throughout this book is that notion that 'if you always do what you always did, you will always get what you always got'. I mentioned the notion of doing things differently and I want to expand on that today. In order to get the most from your developing sense of self, you have to be prepared to do things differently.

Many people would say that it is absolute madness to keep on doing the same thing, time after time, expecting to get a different result or for something different to happen. Alternatively, many people, especially those in the personal development and wellness fields, would describe it as intelligent to have a goal and be wonderfully flexible about how you go about achieving it. You know all about goal setting from our early days.

If what you were doing in the past was not working or increasing your self-esteem as you wanted it to, the answer is simple, do something else.

I was working with a corporate client recently and had been working with a particular senior manager. He had wanted his team to carry out a piece of project work in a certain way. He said to me that he had told them again and again (12 times in total), but they still weren't doing what he wanted. I pointed out that if he wanted them to change what they were doing, he might have to change what he was doing. I suggested that he be more flexible. Together, we explored some alternative approaches and things started to change. Your mind enjoys being stretched and it gets stretched when you do things differently. As you get used to stretching your brain and doing things differently, your self-esteem is going to be tremendously enhanced.

If you are fed up with getting the same results to certain things over and over, with whatever it is that you are looking to change, use this notion to begin to disrupt your existing pattern and get some freshness into your life. If you are just following this idea through in some way, by definition you are perceiving it differently and doing yourself lots of favours. You'll be boosting your self-esteem. As we near the end of this book, it is going to be important to do things differently as you plan to take action and be responsible for your own self-esteem development.

So, firstly, identify an area of your own self-esteem development where you have been doing the same thing over and over hoping to get a different result. It may relate to a behaviour, habit, circumstance or situation; just choose something that you want to change the outcome of.

Then secondly, clarify your goal, that is, clarify what you want to achieve. Do this by asking yourself what you want and how you will know when you have got it. Refer back to the day (all that long time ago) when I was talking about well-formed outcomes here if you need reminding on how to create well-formed outcomes.

Thirdly, construct or create a list of the different approaches and behaviours you have tried, in order to enhance your self-esteem prior to reading this book.

Finally and most simply, put together a nice list of some alternative behaviours you will use to achieve your increased self-esteem, including lots of the elements from this book. This is going to serve you well when you reach the end of this book and have to plan for your future. Enlist some help if you feel it would be beneficial. When you have compiled a good list (put stuff down on that list that may well not seem right for you, it is good to explore avenues that in the past may have made you feel uncomfortable from time to time). Then, of course, look at starting to do the things that are on your list. Go ahead and do them.

What I am wanting to get across here is the idea of being more bendy.

Your mind and your body really are a single system, so it follows that physical flexibility can often lead to greater mental flexibility. There are certain activities which can greatly increase physical flexibility, including things like yoga, martial arts, dancing, swimming and lots of other general forms of exercise.

Practising any of these will increase your overall behavioural and mental flexibility and level of self-esteem. In addition, find opportunities to break habitual patterns. For instance, most mornings when I shave, I do it in a different way. This requires me to stay aware and vary my patterns. The more flexibility you have, the more flexibility you can bring to situations involving others. Often, when people are seeing me for reducing their weight, I might suggest that they look at doing things like swapping their knife and fork hands around for a week.

Here is a list of some things that you can do to interrupt your existing patterns, increase your wellness and boost your brain. You can be as creative as you want with these things.

- Eat a food that you never usually eat.
- Go for a walk at an early hour in the morning.
- Watch a TV show you would never usually watch.
- Take a different journey home from work.
- Take a cold shower.
- Answer your phone with the opposite hand to usual.
- Laugh and smile for no reason.

The sooner you start doing this, the more fun you will have with it. Then the more you also boost your self-esteem. So many people I encounter know all this stuff or read it and still don't do these things and wonder why they are not getting what they want. Do something different today and you will be amazed how your self-esteem rockets.

Project for today: Starting to do things differently starts today. Here is a long and comprehensive exercise to follow called the circle of confidence. Run through the exercise now and see if you can incorporate it into your daily routine.

Circle of Confidence

Get yourself into a comfortable position, just tuning into the idea of using your imagination throughout this exercise. Now whether you see these things, imagine them, or just think 'ok, I know it is there somewhere' just trust that you are doing it in the way that is right for you.

Notice in front of you and imagine a circle on the floor. This circle is yours, your circle of confidence and allows you to create everything you desire to become and be truly confident. Now step into the circle. As you step into the circle, imagine a light is beginning to shine down upon you, integrating a new level of confidence into your reality and into your life. As you are in this circle, just press and hold together the thumb and forefinger of your dominant hand. Squeeze them gently now. This we will call your anchor for confidence.

Each time you step into this circle of confidence you will say certain words and allow them to become your thoughts, your reality and your feelings. Now really imagine this light shining down onto the crown of your head, through your spine and filling your body. As you allow the light to shine down on you, the light illuminates your body and it integrates these learnings in a way that is in harmony with your body and mind. Now step out of the circle and release the anchor.

Look at your circle of confidence, imagine it getting brighter, more vibrant, enriched and more powerful each time you step in. Now step in again, and say the words that follow as they become your reality. Imagine bringing in the light again, imagine it pouring down upon you and press your anchor. Hold that thumb and forefinger together. As the light floats down through your mind and body, you accept the words and allow them to become your reality:

'You love your body – others love your physiology too, from top to toe, you take care of your body, feed it nourishing foods, exercise and keep it strong and healthy. You hold your body, comfortably and purposefully in a way that attracts the right people into your life.' Step out of the circle, release your anchor. Take a deep breath.

Step into the circle, press your anchor together again. As the light floats down through your mind and body, you accept these words and allow them to become your reality. 'You love your attractive, magnetic personality – you care about others, you are interested in others, curious about them, you are a great listener, you are spontaneous and confident in your ability to speak candidly with others, others find that so wonderfully attractive and magnetic, it is a joy to be around.' Step out of the circle, release your anchor. Take a nice deep breath.

Step into the circle, press your anchor together again. As the light floats down through your mind and body, you accept these words and allow them to become your reality. 'You love your way with people – you have a natural smile that coveys your deep confidence, even across the room, you feel a connection reaching out from where you are to those who share your love of confidence and self-esteem.' Step out of the circle, release anchor. Take a deep breath.

Step into the circle, press your anchor together again. As the light floats down through your mind and body, accessing your deeper levels of being, you accept these words and allow them to become your reality. 'You love your ability to connect with others – you have a light around your body, that others sense. They feel a natural attraction to, a desire to be in that light as it feels warm and inviting, wonderfully magnetic. This strength of attraction gets stronger and stronger every day. Others enjoy being in your light and you notice the way they look at you with interest and desire.' Step out of the circle, release your anchor.

Step into the circle, press your anchor together again. As the light floats down through your mind and body, you accept these words and allow them to become your reality. 'You love your magnetic and attractive personality – you are interesting and sometimes fascinating. You are genuinely interested in what others have to say and what they want. You are secure with who you are with a developing sense of self that you exude. Others are attracted to you for who you are and the way you make them feel. Others feel good when they are around you and desire to know you better.' Step out of the circle, release your anchor.

Now step out of the circle and imagine you step into a room filled with interesting people. Notice the way your confident energy projects to others in the room. Like there is a light shining from deep inside you.

It seems now as if they almost sense your presence, your magnetic pull, even your confident scent. You are in your circle of confidence more and more of the time and you can activate your anchor more and more often. The more you practise, the better it gets. Just imagine more and more each day that a beautiful light surrounds you and creates a glowing, magnetic light that you carry around with you wherever you go. The more you think about it, the more powerful it becomes.

Take those good confident feelings and those confident sensations and keep them in the place within you where you know things to be true. Hold these feelings, thoughts and new beliefs deeply within you. When you are sure that you have embedded all those good feelings and soaked up all that amazing confident energy, take a deep breath and relax.

Day Twenty

Live as long as you may, the first twenty years
are the longest half of your life.
Robert Southey, *The Doctor* (1812)

Today I want to introduce you to a very helpful tool; how to reframe.

I get inundated with emails from more and more people telling me about the stress or lack of self-esteem in their lives, those people could all do with some useful information on reframing. Usually I advise them of this kind of information. This is one way to enhance your day-to-day experiences all the time.

As I have mentioned before, I used to work for the Independent National newspaper in Canary Wharf, London. I can remember in the build up to Christmas, my department was having a large and expensive new computer system installed because the newspaper was being re-launched. It was when Andrew Marr and Rosie Boycott were becoming joint editors; I digress. The system was being put in just before Christmas, but it was a massive task, with numerous issues and overruns. As Christmas approached, there were still a number of teething problems, which led to stretched relations between the system supplier and the newspaper staff.

At one meeting about the integration of the system, my director had been trying to get more time investment from the installation company, only to be told that their people weren't going to be available on Christmas day. My director was frustrated and furious, asking 'what are you doing that's more important than sorting out our system?' Without hesitating, the guy from the installation company said 'delivering Christmas hampers to the elderly'. The impact was immediate; everyone in the room started laughing and my director joined them, realising that he had perhaps been a bit unreasonable. Everyone knew that the story about the elderly was not true, but that did not matter – the statement had changed his perception of the situation, instantly, and he started behaving more reasonably.

Changing the Contextual Frame

There was an advertisement for the Guardian newspaper here in the UK, which showed a set of still photographs arranged in a particular action sequence. The photographs showed a large framed man with very little hair on his head, wearing jeans and boots, running along a pathway with a real purpose.

In the first frame he is running towards an elderly lady. In the second frame, you see him knock her violently into the street. In the third frame you see him make his escape, obviously and seemingly this is another thug terrorising the elderly.

Then, when you turn the page, you are presented with some wider angle shots. In the wide-angle shots, you see the elderly lady casually walking beside a building that has building works being carried out upon it and where a cement mixer is about to topple from a scaffold. An alert pedestrian notices the situation and heroically runs towards the lady, pushing her clear of the building area. A moment later, the cement mixer falls to the ground in the spot where the lady was standing. The initially perceived 'thug' has in fact saved her life.

By changing the frame, the creators of the advertisement had changed the context of the man's actions. Suddenly, what was perceived as typically criminal then became valiant and altruistic. His actions were transformed in a moment as they were reframed. I am sure you know of many other examples of this.

One of the things I have learnt over the years from one of the main fields I work in and something that fascinates and tests me, is that every behaviour is useful or valuable in some context. Upon learning and reading about this in the embryonic days of my learning, I did do my best to do the opposite! I wracked my brains for things that I just could not reframe. Of course, I could not do so for long. It's just a matter of stretching your brain and finding a context that makes it useful. I have not always found this easy. This process is referred to as context reframing.

Every Behaviour is Useful in the Right Context

Now here is a challenge for you. For any behaviour, no matter how frustrating or apparently without use or value, see if you can find a context where it is useful. Once you find such a context, a subsequent act of presenting the behaviour in a new light is reframing it. Simple eh? If it was originally a behaviour that was treated very seriously or was problematic, you may then also want to think about adding humour or some playfulness in the way you re-present it.

So firstly, identify a complaint that you may have either about yourself or someone else, a simple structured one to begin with, for example; 'I'm too [x]' or 'She's too [y]' (i.e. 'I'm too impatient', 'He's too selfish', 'She's too messy').

Then secondly, identify to yourself in what contexts would the characteristic being complained about have value and usefulness. How can you take this complaint and make it useful or beneficial in some way?

Thirdly, create several answers to this question, and then craft it into a 'reframe'. This reframe is then going to be how you choose to observe what used to be a complaint about yourself. This way, you stop complaining and start being more progressive about yourself and building yourself up. You are actually adding more to that ever growing list of things you like about yourself, remember that?

So for example, someone might say 'I'm too impatient' about themselves. A nice way to reframe it would be to say 'I bet you're quick-thinking in an emergency'.

The complaint of 'she's too messy' can be reframed into 'she'd be good to have around if we were trying to make our home look like it had been burgled'. I don't like to be too serious about these things!

'He's too selfish' can be reframed as 'we've had so many problems with people not taking care of themselves, it's often good to make sure you look after yourself to be in a better position to help others'.

Now, I know these are a bit lame, but they do not have to be that useful at this stage. It is more important that you give yourself the freedom to be creative so your brain gets the pattern of what you are doing. What's more, when you have to do that and develop better reframes for yourself, your learning is far more comprehensive than if I were to spoon feed you responses to regurgitate.

The next important step in our self-esteem development then is to come up with reframes for all the complaints that you have about yourself. This can be a lot of fun if you do it with someone else (i.e. you say 'I'm too [x]' and they generate reframes).

By the way, the example of 'I'm too sexy' as in the 90s Pop Band 'Right Said Fred' chart topping hit is not really appropriate.

The fifth step is that once you get the hang of it, start looking for opportunities to use context reframing each day with yourself to develop more self-esteem. You can start with the less challenging ones and advance as you get better at doing this.

So finally, for these initial steps of reframing, write a list of the complaints that you have had about yourself in the past and generate a number of context reframes for each one. Then, look forward with a sense of anticipation to the next time you or someone else reminds you of that old complaint. Please bear in mind that you are opening up options here, not covering things up, if a particular problematic issue is occurring, sometimes it may not be appropriate to just reframe.

Both my Grandparents on my father's side were 80 a few years ago and we had celebratory family gatherings. As I walked into one of the celebrations I asked the standard question 'So, what's it like waking up on your 80th birthday, Grandad?' To which he replied 'better than not waking up on your 80th birthday'. Good reframe.

Now, I want to start playing with 'content reframing'. If a footballer kicks the ball into his team's net, it's called an 'own goal', but if a soldier accidentally shoots one of his fellow soldiers, it's called 'friendly fire'. Sounds kind of cuddly, doesn't it? But you would not want any coming your way. George Orwell's 1984 had plenty of examples of content reframing i.e. the ministries of peace and truth that live on today in many forms, a peacekeeper missile, anyone?

So, content reframing involves changing the meaning of something.

Right, to develop this further, follow this procedure; identify a complaint or issue with the structure 'I feel [x] when [y] happens'.

For example, 'I feel lacking in confidence when he laughs at me' or 'I feel embarrassed when speaking to groups of people'.

Next, ask yourself 'what else could this (y) mean?', 'What else could this (x) mean?' or 'what else could this situation mean?', or ask 'how can this (x) or (y) be interpreted?'

Then, you can come up with several answers to these and then create a 'reframe'.

For example, a complaint could be 'I feel upset when I see the mess these kids have made' and the reframe could be 'It's good that they can enjoy themselves fully without worrying about a few things being out of place.'

Alternate example reframe, 'A little untidiness is a small price to pay for happy children.'

Another example reframe, 'The fact that it's messy means they're expressing their creativity.'

As with my previous examples, these are not the most amazing reframes in the world, but they don't have to be that useful at this stage. It is more important that you give yourself the freedom to be creative so your brain gets the pattern of what you are doing. This will evolve into being a very valuable daily tool to enhance how you feel about yourself and your life.

Then, once you get the hang of it, start looking for opportunities to use content reframing each day. For spreading good feelings around and helping people to lessen the way that they can get 'bogged down' in the trivial sometimes. Trivial things can often consume us without us being aware of it.

Once again, in a business sense, content reframing is also very powerful for dealing with objections of all sorts. For example, a reframe I sometimes use when someone objects to the price of consulting with me (I am so expensive!) is to respond with something along the lines of:

'If you are after a cheap consultant or therapist, then I am not the right consultant for you. If however, you want to invest in your future then maybe I am. If your child needed a serious operation, would you look for the cheapest surgeon? Then why look for the cheapest way to make changes in your life that are important enough to seek help with?'

Again, I do have my tongue planted in my cheek as I write that riposte, however, I am sure you see where I am coming from here.

Then finally, list the objections you get most frequently and generate a number of content reframes for each one. Then, look forward with a sense of anticipation to the next time someone offers that objection.

Project for today: Write a list of complaints that you used to have about yourself and reframe them as progressively and beneficially as you possibly can. Run the reframes over and over in your mind until you get them firmly embedded in your mind and they have become your true perception of yourself.

Day Twenty-One

Keep your face turned towards the light, and the
shadows of doubt will always be behind.

Anon.

Planning for Your Future Filled with Self-Esteem

Today's quote was nothing to do with the days number, it is representative of how you move forward from here. Today is a short day because you want to create, plot, plan and design what you are going to do every day to create your successful and confidence filled existence. Do this by putting together a six month strategic self-esteem plan.

As of now, you have all the techniques, skills, resources, beliefs and equipped with your life experience, your dreams and expectations you can now make your intentions clear to yourself about where you are going to go from here. Assess what you have learnt and how you are going to apply it.

You want to create a life filled with self-esteem, self-worth, value and confidence and therefore if you construct your plan for the future correctly, you will achieve that.

You don't want to learn all of these things in theory and just let them sit dormant within you; you need to take continued action to build upon the previous 20 days of learning. Instead use lots of varying strategies to be really effective.

Within your six month plan, write down what you are going to do each and every day and make sure it gets done. The momentum you build will serve to motivate you and make you do more and more. It is important that each and every day you contribute to enhancing your self-esteem. Do something every day, even if it is a daily routine of assessing all the good things about your day.

Read through this book again and again and carry out all the aspects of it, put them in your plan at certain days and continue to measure what yields the most success for you. Then do those things more and alter how you have been doing the other things. If you persist with the various strategies and learnings in this book, having high levels of self-esteem is a close certainty.

I wish you all the very best wishes and trust that you will allow yourself to enjoy the journey. You deserve it.

Project for today: Write a 6 month day by day plan as to what strategies you are going to employ to ensure that you build and develop your self-esteem as if today is a new beginning, because it is.

Bibliography

Andreas, Connirae and Steve
Heart of The Mind
(Real People Press; November 1989)

Cameron-Bandler, Leslie et al.
Know How: Guided Programs for Inventing Your Own Best Future
(Futurepace; January 1986)

Covey, Stephen
Seven Habits of Highly Effective People
(Free Press; 1st edition 15 September 1990)

Dilts, Robert
Applications of Neuro Linguistic Programming
(Meta Publications; 1983)

Dilts, Robert
From Coach to Awakener
(Meta Pubns; May 2003)

Eason, Adam
The Secrets of Self-Hypnosis
(Network 3000 Publishing; August 2005)

Hall, Michael & Bodenhamer, Bob
The Users Manual for the Brain
(Crown House Publishing; Revised edition; 1 January 2001)

Hill, Napoleon
Think and Grow Rich
(Ballantine Books; Reissue edition 12 May 1987)

Hogan, Kevin
Irresistible Attraction,
(Network 3000; 1st edition 7 June 2000)

Hogan, Kevin
The Psychology of Persuasion
(Pelican Publishing Company; May 1996)

Jeffers, Susan
Feel the Fear and Do It Anyway
(Ballantine Books; Reissue edition 12 April 1988)

Maltz, Maxwell
Psycho-Cybernetics
(Pocket; Reprint edition 15 August 1989)

Maslow, Abraham
Motivation and Personality
(NY: Harper; 1954)

McKenna, Paul
Change Your Life in Seven Days
(Bantam Press; 21 December 2003)

Orwell, George
1984
(Signet Classics; Reissue edition 1 July 1950)

Robbins, Anthony
Unlimited Power
(Free Press; Reprint edition 22 December 1997)

Rogers, Carl
Client Centred Therapy
(Houghton Mifflin College Div; June 1951)

Adam Eason

Adam Eason is a prodigious talent in the world of hypnosis and personal development. One of the most qualified in his field, highly academically recognised as an international best selling author, motivational speaker, therapist, consultant and trainer in the fields of hypnosis, communication, personal development and human potential. Adam has worked with thousands of individuals, has featured in international, national and local media and appeared on television on numerous occasions including starring in the primetime BBC1 TV programme 'Run for Glory' using his techniques to help participants overcome psychological barriers to achievement. He brings a refreshingly ready wit and contagious enthusiasm that permeates all of his work and spreads to all who experience it.

Eager to demonstrate the array of benefits of the varying techniques he employs, Adam has a passion for leading by example and personal experience. His competitive nature is amply demonstrated by successfully competing in marathon, half marathon and various other running events as well as with the successful businesses he runs.

Adam has worked with many of the worlds most famous trainers in the field of human potential, and continues to be a student in these fascinating fields. Continually researching, studying and working toward discovering and understanding human happiness, achievement and excellence. Adam encourages innovation by seeking out and employing cutting edge technologies from across the world.

Those who have seen him speak, invested in his programmes, consulted with him and attended his seminars continue to be moved deeply; they learn profoundly and laugh loudly.

www.adam-eason.com

Printed in the United States
103726LV00002B/36/A